2023

Wiley

CPA
EXAM REVIEW

FOCUS NOTES

Wiley 2023 CPA EXAM REVIEW

FOCUS NOTES

BUSINESS ENVIRONMENT AND CONCEPTS

WILEY

CONTENTS

v

Contents   vi

Contents

Contents   viii

PREFACE

This publication is a comprehensive yet simplified study program. It provides a review of the basic skills and concepts tested on the CPA exam, and teaches important strategies to take the exam faster and more accurately. This tool allows you to take control of the CPA exam.

This simplified and focused approach to studying for the CPA exam can be used:

- As a handy and convenient reference manual
- To solve exam questions
- To reinforce material being studied

Included is critical information necessary to obtain a passing score on the CPA exam in a concise and easy-to-use format. Due to the wide variety of information covered on the exam, a number of techniques are included:

- Acronyms and mnemonics to help you learn and remember a variety of rules and checklists
- Formulas and equations that simplify complex calculations required on the exam
- Simplified outlines of key concepts without the details that encumber or distract from learning the essential elements

- Techniques that can be applied to problem solving or essay writing, such as preparing a multiple-step income statement, determining who will prevail in a legal conflict, or developing an audit program
- Pro forma statements, reports, and schedules that make it easy to prepare these items by simply filling in the blanks
- Proven techniques to help you become a smarter, sharper, and more accurate test taker

This publication may also be useful to university students enrolled in Intermediate, Advanced, and Cost Accounting classes; Auditing, Business Law, and Federal Income Tax classes; or Economics and Finance classes.

CORPORATE GOVERNANCE AND INTERNAL CONTROL

Corporate Rights, Responsibilities, and Authority

Corporate Governance: Establish Incentives and Monitoring

- Owners separate from management
- Agency problem: Will managers act in owners' interest?

Incentives to Defeat Agency Problem

Forms of Executive Compensation

- Base salary and profit: Usually based on accounting measures
  - May lead to earnings manipulation or taking excessive risk

Incentives to Defeat Agency Problem (continued)

- Stock options: align shareholders' and managers' interest in increasing share prices
  - Differences in timing horizons (management short term?)
  - Underwater options provide no incentive
- Restricted stock: force managers to think long term

Monitoring Devices

- Boards of directors
  - Independent nominating/corporate governance committee
  - Independent audit committee (AC) under Sarbanes-Oxley (SOX)
    - At least one financial expert
    - External auditors must report directly to AC
    - AC appoints, determines compensation, and oversees external auditor

Focus on
Corporate Governance and Internal Control

2

Incentives to Defeat Agency Problem (continued)

- Stock exchange rules
  - Majority independent directors
    - Provide information to investors as to who is independent
  - Have a code of conduct and make it available
  - Have an independent AC (required by SOX)
  - Have an independent compensation committee (required by Dodd-Frank)
  - Clawback rules that require executives to pay back incentive compensation when there is an accounting restatement (required by Dodd-Frank)
  - Nonbinding shareholder votes on executive compensation and golden parachutes (required by Dodd-Frank)

Focus on

Corporate Governance and Internal Control

3

Incentives to Defeat Agency Problem (continued)

- Internal auditors

  - Provide assurance on risk management and internal control
  - Should report at least indirectly to AC

    - Independent and competent
    - Chief IC officer reports directly to CEO
    - Should adhere to Institute of Internal Auditors (IIA) professional and ethical standards. These standards apply to both individual auditors and internal audit departments.

- External auditors

  - Help assure users that financials are accurate and not fraudulent
  - Must attest to management's assessment of effective internal control as required by SOX
  - The Jumpstart Our Business Startups (JOBS) Act exempted "emerging growth companies" for a maximum of five years from the date of their initial public offering from certain requirements that apply to larger public companies, including external reporting on internal control

Incentives to Defeat Agency Problem (continued)

- SEC and SOX
  - CEO and CFO must certify accuracy and truthfulness with criminal penalties
  - Fraud in sale or purchase of securities punishable by fine and/or prison
  - Destruction or other damage to documentation to hinder investigation punishable by fine and/or prison
  - Retaliation on "whistleblowers" punishable by fine and/or prison

17 Principles of Internal Control

Internal Controls

COSO: Internal Control Integrated Framework (Revised 2013)

Internal control is defined by COSO as a process, effected by the entity's board of directors, management, and other personnel, designed to provide reasonable assurance regarding the achievement of objectives relating to operations, reporting, and compliance. It has five components and 17 principles.

1. The **control environment** is the set of standards, processes, and structures that provide the basis for carrying out internal control across the organization. Principles include:

    a. Commitment to integrity and ethical values.
    b. The board of directors demonstrates independence from management and exercises oversight.
    c. Management establishes structures, reporting lines, and appropriate authorities and responsibilities in the pursuit of objectives.
    d. Commitment to attract, develop and retain competent individuals.
    e. Hold individuals accountable for their internal control responsibilities.

Internal Controls (continued)

2. **Risk assessment** is management's process for identifying, analyzing, and responding to risks. Principles include:

   a. Specify objectives with sufficient clarity to enable the identification and assessment of risks.

   b. Identify risks to the achievement of its objectives and analyze risks as a basis for determining how the risks should be managed.

   c. Consider the potential for fraud.

   d. Identify and assess changes that could significantly impact internal control.

3. **Control activities** are policies and procedures that help ensure that management directives are carried out. Principles include:

   a. Select and develop control activities that contribute to the mitigation of risks.

   b. Select and develop general control activities over technology to support the achievement of objectives.

   c. Deploy control activities through policies that establish what is expected and procedures that put policies into action.

Internal Controls (continued)

Control activities to mitigate risks include:

a. Authorizations and approvals

b. Verifications

c. Physical controls

d. Controls over standing data

e. Reconciliations

f. Supervisory controls

Internal Controls (continued)

4. The **information and communication** component of internal control supports all of the other components. Principles include:

   a. The organization obtains or generates and uses relevant, quality information to support the functioning of internal control.

   b. The organization internally communicates information, including objectives and responsibilities for internal control.

   c. The organization communicates with external parties regarding matters affecting the functioning of internal control.

5. **Monitoring activities** assess whether each of the five components is present and functioning. Principles include:

   a. Select, develop, and perform ongoing and/or separate evaluations to ascertain whether the components of internal control are present and functioning.

   b. Evaluate and communicate internal control deficiencies in a timely manner to those parties responsible for taking corrective action.

Limitations of and Deficiencies in Accounting Controls

Limitations of Internal Control

A. Internal control is management's responsibility. Management's objectives may lead to poor controls.

B. Internal control depends heavily on people.

C. Management may be able to, and may choose to, override internal control.

D. Collusion is an important risk in internal control systems.

E. Bad stuff happens. External events beyond the organization's control may lead to control failures.

F. Inherent limitations, such as those just listed, preclude an internal control system from providing absolute assurance.

Deficiencies in Internal Control

A. An **internal control deficiency** is a shortcoming in a component or components that reduces the likelihood of an entity achieving its objectives.

B. Types of internal control deficiencies:

    a. **Control deficiency:** defined above. This is the least serious of the three types of control deficiencies.

    b. **Significant deficiency:** A deficiency (or combination of deficiencies) in internal control that is *more serious than a control deficiency* but *less severe than a material weakness*, yet it is important enough to merit attention by those charged with governance.

    c. **Material weakness:** A deficiency (or combination of deficiencies) in internal control such that there is a reasonable possibility that a *material misstatement* of the entity's financial statements will not be prevented or detected and corrected on a timely basis. A material misstatement of financial statements means that decisions of someone who relies on the statements could be wrong because of the misstatement. Hence, a material weakness is really bad.

Categories of Controls

Preventive, Detective, and Corrective Controls

This classification focuses on the **timing of the control relative to the potential error**. A well-controlled system balances preventive and detective controls and includes corrective controls as needed.

1. **Preventive controls—"before-the-fact" controls:** Preventive controls attempt to **stop an error or irregularity before it occurs.**

2. **Detective controls—"after-the-fact" controls:** Detective controls attempt to **detect an error after it has occurred.**

3. **Corrective controls are always paired with detective controls.** Corrective controls attempt to reverse the effects of the observed error or irregularity. Examples of corrective controls include maintenance of backup files, disaster recovery plans, and insurance.

Feedback and Feedforward Controls

Feedback and feedforward controls focus on changing inputs or processes to promote desirable outcomes by comparing actual results (feedback) or projected results feedforward to a predetermined standard.

1. **Feedback controls:** Evaluate the results of a process and, if the results are undesirable, adjust the process to correct the results; most detective controls are also feedback controls.

2. **Feedforward controls:** Project future results based on current and past information and, if the future results are undesirable, change the inputs to the system to prevent the outcome. Inventory ordering systems are examples of feedforward controls.

General Controls and Application Controls

This classification focuses on **where** the control is applied rather than **when** it is applied.

1. **General controls:** Controls over the entire environment (i.e., "umbrella" controls). They apply to all functions, not just specific accounting applications.

   Examples: Restricting physical access to computer resources, production and storage of backup files, and performing background checks of computer services personnel

2. **Application controls:** Controls over specific **data input, data processing, and data output** activities. **Application controls** are sometimes called "transaction controls" since they relate specifically to transaction processing.

   Examples: Checks to ensure that input data is complete and properly formatted (e.g., dates, dollar amounts), that account numbers are valid, and that values are reasonable (e.g., that we don't sell quantities that are greater than the quantity currently in inventory).

Focus on

Corporate Governance and Internal Control

Internal Control Monitoring Purpose and Terminology

How Does Monitoring Benefit Corporate Governance?

Monitoring is the core, underlying control component in the COSO ERM model.

Why Is Control Monitoring Important?

- People forget, quit jobs, get lazy, or come to work hungover; machines fail. Over time, controls deteriorate.

- Advances in technology and management techniques demand that internal control and related monitoring processes continually evolve and improve.

Control Monitoring Terminology

Who evaluates controls? **Evaluators** monitor internal control. Two primary attributes of effective evaluators are **competence** and **objectivity**.

Competence: The evaluator's knowledge of the controls and related processes, including how controls should operate and what constitutes a control deficiency.

Objectivity: Objectivity concerns the extent to which the evaluator may be influenced by personal or vested interests in the outcome of the evaluation.

Levels of Monitoring

Board monitoring: Control monitoring by the board, its committees, or others charged with overseeing management conduct

Self-assessment: Occurs when persons responsible for a unit or function determine the effectiveness of controls for their activities

Self-review: Refers to the review of one's own work

Nature or Quality of Controls

Control objectives: Specific targets against which the effectiveness of internal control is evaluated

Compensating controls: Controls that accomplish the same objective as another control and that can be expected to "compensate" for deficiencies in that control

Deficiency or internal control deficiency: A condition within an internal control system requiring attention

Nature or Quality of Controls *(continued)*

Key controls: Those controls that are most important to concluding about the ability of the internal control system to manage or mitigate meaningful risks

Key performance indicators: Metrics that reflect critical success factors. They help organizations measure progress toward goals and objectives.

Key risk indicators (KRIs)—Forward-looking metrics that seek to identify potential problems, thus enabling an organization to take timely action, if necessary.

Fraud Risk Management

What Is Fraud?

1. COSO defines fraud as "any intentional act or omission designed to deceive others, resulting in the victim suffering a loss and/or the perpetrator achieving a gain."

2. COSO identifies four categories of fraud:

   a. **Reporting fraud—financial:** An intentional misstatement of accounting information

   b. **Reporting fraud—nonfinancial:** Manipulating nonfinancial reports, including environmental, health, safety, production, quality, or customer reports

   c. **Misappropriation of assets:** Theft or misuse of tangible or intangible assets by employees, customers, vendors, hackers, or criminal organizations

   d. **Other illegal acts and corruption:** Violations of laws or regulations that may have a material impact on the financial statements

3. **IT and Fraud:** IT can both facilitate fraud and help prevent and detect fraud.

Fraud Risk Management Principles

Principle 1—Control Environment. The organization establishes and communicates a fraud risk management program that demonstrates the expectations of the board of directors and senior management and their commitment to high integrity and ethical values regarding managing fraud risk.

Principle 2—Risk Assessment. The organization performs comprehensive fraud risk assessments to identify specific fraud schemes and risks, assess their likelihood and significance, evaluate existing fraud control activities, and implements actions to mitigate residual fraud risks.

Principle 3—Control Activities. The organization selects, develops, and deploys preventive and detective fraud control activities to mitigate the risk of fraud events occurring or not being detected in a timely manner.

Fraud Risk Management Principles (continued)

Principle 4—Information and Communication. The organization establishes a communication process to obtain information about potential fraud and deploys a coordinated approach to investigation and corrective action to address fraud.

Principle 5—Monitoring Activities. The organization selects, develops, and performs ongoing evaluations to ascertain the presence of the five principles of fraud risk management and functioning and communicates the fraud risk management program deficiencies in a timely manner to parties responsible for taking corrective action, including senior management and the board of directors.

The COSO ERM Model

Enterprise Risk Management: Eight Components

1. Internal environment (tone of the organization)
   a. Effective board
   b. Ethical management
   c. Risk appetite: How much risk is an organization willing to accept to achieve a goal?
   d. Risk tolerance: How far above or below meeting the objective is allowable?
2. Objective setting
   a. Well-defined mission
   b. Process to set objectives that align with goals
3. Event identification
   a. Internal
      1) Loss of key personnel
      2) Damage to infrastructure (e.g., IS crash)
      3) Key product/process becomes obsolete

Focus on
Corporate Governance and Internal Control

Enterprise Risk Management: Eight Components (continued)

    b. External

        1)   Establish "trigger points" (e.g., competition increases market share above x amount)

        2)   Process to assess demographic and economic changes

    c. Black swan analysis: Evaluate negative events that were unforeseen to determine why they occurred

4. Risk assessment: What are the risks?

    a. Assess impact and probability

    b. Inherent risk: What if management does nothing in response to identified risk?

    c. Residual risk: residual after management's response

Enterprise Risk Management: Eight Components (continued)

5. Risk responses

    a. Avoidance

    b. Reduction

    c. Sharing

    d. Acceptance

6. Control activities: Policies and procedures to insure that risk responses are implemented

7. Information and communication throughout organization

    a. Organization's objectives

    b. Risk appetite and tolerance

    c. Role of ERM in managing risk

8. Monitoring: Effective process to oversee ERM

Enterprise Risk Management: Limitations

1. The future is uncertain
2. No absolute assurances
   a. Human failure
   b. System breakdown
   c. Collusion across ERM
   d. Management override

Introduction to Enterprise Risk Management

What Is Enterprise Risk Management?

Enterprise risk management (ERM) is the culture, capabilities, and practices by which organizations manage risk to create, preserve, and realize value (performance).

Risk is an uncertain event that will influence whether an organization achieves its strategic business goals.

1. A **negative risk** is that the new accounting system that your company implemented fails to work and you cannot keep track of sales and inventory (e.g., the 1999 Hershey's Chocolate enterprise risk planning disaster).

2. A **positive risk** might be that your company's servers fail because demand for your project is so high (which occurred repeatedly in the early days of eBay).

Managing ERM

Managing ERM includes a focus on these six elements of an organization:

1. **Entity culture.** An organization's culture is the way that people in the organization think and behave.
2. **Developing capabilities.** Organizations must hire, foster, promote, and nurture skills and competence.
3. **Adaptation and integration of ERM practices.** ERM is dynamic; it requires adaptation to special projects, new initiatives, and innovative technologies.
4. **Integrating with strategy setting and performance.** ERM must be integrated with an organization's strategy, mission, and performance goals.
5. **Managing risk related to strategy and business objectives.** Well-designed and implemented ERM provides an entity with a "reasonable expectation" of achieving strategic goals.
6. **Linking to value through risk appetite.** ERM occurs relative to an organization's risk appetite. The organization's risk appetite is reflected in its mission, values, and strategy.

Why Is ERM Important?

What is the organizational value of ERM?

Expanding opportunities: Considering risk enables management to identify new opportunities and the challenges of existing opportunities.

Identifying and managing entity-wide risk: Identifying and managing risk at an entity level enables the consideration of interactions of risks across the entity and of their unique effects on segments or portions of the entity.

Increasing positive and reducing negative outcomes: By better identifying and managing risks, ERM enables entities to achieve superior performance.

Reducing performance variability: ERM enables the assessment of risk performance variability and taking actions to reduce undesirable variance.

Better deployment of assets (and human resources): Every risk demands resources. Better risk assessment and response enable superior resource allocations.

Increasing enterprise resilience: Organizational survival depends on anticipating and responding to changing risks. ERM improves survivability and organizational resilience.

Basic ERM Concepts and Terms

Entity: Any form of for-profit, not-for-profit, or governmental body. In the COSO ERM framework, ERM pronouncement entities are sometimes called organizations and sometimes called businesses.

Event: An incident (occurrence) or set of incidents.

Risk appetite: The types and amount of risk that an organization is willing to accept in pursuit of value. Risk appetite is discussed more completely in the next lesson.

Severity: A measure of the likelihood and impact of events. May also refer to the time required to recover from events.

Uncertainty: The state of not knowing how or if potential events may occur.

ERM Mission, Vision, Values, and Strategy

ERM begins with an entity's mission, vision, values, and strategy. These are described next.

Mission: Why the entity exists, that is, its core purpose. The mission states what the entity wants to achieve.

Vision: The entity's aspirations for its future. The vision states what the organization wants to achieve and be known for and as.

Core values: The entity's beliefs and ideals about morality—what is good or bad, acceptable or unacceptable. Core values influence the behavior of individuals and organizations.

Strategy: The organization's plan to achieve its mission and vision and apply its core values.

Risk and Strategy Selection

Three key risks in strategy selection and implementation are described below.

Risk 1: Misalignment. Does our strategy align with our mission, vision, and core values?

Risk 2: Implications. Do we understand the risk implications of our chosen strategy?

Risk 3 (the least important of the three risks): Risks to Success. Will we be successful? Will we achieve the goals specified in our strategy?

ERM Components, Principles, and Terms

COSO's Risk Management Framework

The five components of the ERM framework are:

1. **Governance and Culture:** These are the cornerstones of the other ERM components. Governance is the allocation of roles, authorities, and responsibilities among stakeholders, the board, and management. An organization's culture is an organization's core values, including how the organization understands and manages risk.

2. **Strategy and Objective Setting:** ERM must integrate with strategic planning and objective setting.

3. **Performance:** Risk identification and assessment are concerned with developing an organization's ability to achieve its strategy and business objectives, as measured by performance.

4. **Review and Revision:** The periodic and continuous review and revision of ERM processes enables an organization to increase the value of its ERM function.

5. **Information, Communication, and Reporting:** Communication is the continual, iterative process of obtaining and sharing information to facilitate and enhance ERM.

Additional Key ERM Terms

Assumption: An assertion (belief) about a characteristic of the future that underlies an organization's ERM plan. For example, a business might assume that the demand for routers will not change substantially.

Bot: A software application that runs automated (usually simple) tasks (scripts) on the internet. Bots to search a website (e.g., eBay, airlines) for bargains are examples. Also called an internet bot or web robot.

Business context: The trends, events, relationships, and other factors that may influence, clarify, or change an entity's current and future strategy and business objectives.

Culture: An entity's core values, including its attitudes, behaviors, and understanding about risk.

Governance: The allocation of roles, authorities, and responsibilities among stakeholders, the board, and management.

Key performance indicator (KPI): A high-level measure of historical performance of an entity and/or its major units.

Key risk indicator (KRI): A leading (predictive) indicator of emerging risks.

Additional Key ERM Terms (continued)

Practices: The methods and approaches deployed within an entity relating to managing risk.

Portfolio view: A composite view of risk the entity faces. Having such a view positions management and the board to consider the types, severity, and interdependencies of risks and how they may affect the entity's performance relative to its strategy and business objectives.

Risk capacity: The maximum amount of risk that an entity can absorb in the pursuit of strategy and business objectives.

Risk ceiling: The maximum level of risk established by an entity.

Risk floor: The minimum level of risk established by an entity.

Risk inventory: A listing of an entity's known risks.

Additional Key ERM Terms *(continued)*

Risk owners: Managers or employees who are accountable for the effective management of identified risks

Risk profile: A composite view of the risk assumed at the entity level; or an aspect of the business that positions management to consider the types, severity, and interdependencies of risks, and how they may affect performance relative to the strategy and business objectives.

Risk range: The acceptable level of risk (highest to lowest) established by the organization.

Target risk: The desired level of risk set by an entity.

Tolerance: The boundaries of acceptable variation in performance related to achieving business objectives.

ERM Governance and Culture—Principles 1–5

1. **Exercise board risk oversight:** The board of directors provides oversight of the strategy and carries out governance responsibilities to support management in achieving strategy and business objectives.

2. **Establish operating structures:** The organization establishes operating structures that support the strategy and business objectives.

3. **Define desired culture:** The board of directors and management define (and exhibit) the desired behaviors that characterize the entity's desired culture.

4. **Demonstrate commitment to core values:** The organization demonstrates a commitment to its core values.

5. **Attract, develop, and retain capable individuals:** The organization is committed to building human capital that aligns with its strategy and business objectives.

ERM Strategy and Objective Setting—Principles 6–7

6. **Analyze the business context:** The "business context" consists of the trends, events, relationships and other factors that may influence, clarify, or change an entity's strategy and business objectives.

   The **external environment,** and stakeholders, influence the business context.

   The **internal environment** consists of influences on strategy and business objectives from within.

7. **Define risk appetite:** The organization defines risk appetite in the context of creating, preserving, and realizing value.

   Determine risk appetite: Management and the board must make an informed choice of an appropriate risk appetite.

   Use risk appetite: Risk appetite guides an organization's resource allocations, including those to its operating units.

ERM Strategy and Objective Setting—Principles 8–10

8. **Evaluate alternative strategies:** The organization evaluates alternative strategies and their potential impact on the risk profile. The strategy must align with the mission, vision, and core values and with the organization's risk appetite.

9. **Formulate business objectives:** The organization considers risk while establishing the business objectives at various levels that align and support strategy.

   Understand and use tolerance: Tolerance is the acceptance range of variation in performance.

ERM Performance, Review, and Communication—Principles 10–11

10. **Identify risk:** The organization identifies risk that impacts the performance of strategy and business objectives.

    Please note that precise risk statements are preferred to vague risk statements.

11. **Assess severity of risk:** The organization assesses the severity of risk.

    a. The severity of risks should be assessed at multiple levels. Risks at higher levels (i.e., that influence strategy and entity-wide objectives) are more likely to influence the entity's overall reputation and brand than risks that occur at lower levels (e.g., to a business unit's objectives).

    b. Risk assessment should consider:

       i. Inherent risk (i.e., the risk in the absence of efforts to address it).

       ii. Target residual risk (i.e., the desired amount of risk after actions to address it).

       iii. Actual residual risk (i.e., the realized risk after taking actions to address it).

12. **Prioritize risks:** The organization prioritizes risks as a basis for selecting risk responses. Prioritization assesses risk severity compared to risk appetite.

   a. Greater priority (importance) may be given to risks that are likely to approach or exceed risk appetite.

   b. Criteria for risk priority may include:

       i. Adaptability—the capacity of the entity to respond to risks

       ii. Complexity—the scope and nature of a risk to the entity's success

       iii. Velocity—the speed at which a risk impacts an entity

       iv. Persistence—the period over which risk impacts the entity

       v. Recovery—the capacity of the entity to return to tolerance

13. **Implement risk response:** The organization identifies and selects risk responses. Acceptable risk response categories include:

Accept: No action is taken to change the severity of the risk.

Avoid: Act to remove the risk, which may mean, for example, ceasing a product line, declining to expand to a new geographical market, or selling a division.

Pursue: Accept increased risk to achieve improved performance.

Reduce: Act to reduce the severity of the risk.

Share: Reduce the severity of the risk by transferring or sharing a portion of it.

14. **Develop portfolio view:** The organization develops and evaluates a portfolio view of risk.

Using the portfolio view of risk enables an organization to identity risks that are severe at the entity level.

Multiple, acceptable methods exist for creating a portfolio view of risk.

15. **Assess substantial change:** The organization identifies and assesses changes that may substantially affect strategy and business objectives.

    Examples of internal substantial changes include rapid growth, innovation, and major changes in leadership or personnel.

    Examples of external substantial changes include increased competitive pressures and changes in operating requirements.

16. **Review risk and performance:** The organization reviews entity performance and considers related risks.

    Periodically, organizations must review their ERM capabilities and practices. Such reviews seek answers to questions such as:

    How has the entity performed?

    What risks influence performance?

Monitoring, Review, and Revision—ERM Principles 16–17 (continued)

Is the entity taking sufficient risk to attain its target?

Were risk estimates accurate?

17. **Pursue ERM improvement:** The organization pursues improvement of its ERM activities and functions.

ERM Communication and Reporting—Principle 18

18. **Leverage information systems:** The organization leverages the entity's information and technology systems to support ERM.

   Relevant information may be structured (organized and searchable) or unstructured (unstructured and disorganized).

   Effective data management includes three key elements:

   a. *Data and information governance* includes governance processes for identifying data and risk owners and holding them accountable.
   b. *Processes and controls* help an entity create and maintain reliable data.
   c. *Data management architecture* refers to the fundamental design of the technology and related data.

19. **Communicate risk information:** The organization uses communication channels to support ERM.

    Communication between the board and management begins with a shared understanding of the entity's strategy and business objectives.

20. **Report on risk, culture, and performance:** The organization reports on risk, culture, and performance at multiple levels and across the entity.

    Key risk indicators (KRIs) measure emerging risks.

    KRIs are often reported with key performance indicators (KPIs), which provide high-level measures of organizational performance.

Practical Steps for Starting an Enterprise Risk Management (ERM) Initiative

Key to success: Integrate ERM into existing governance activities (as opposed to creating new activities and processes).

7 Key "Theme Activities" for Success in Starting ERM

1. Start at the top and secure board of directors' and management support.
2. Clearly communicate role and objectives of ERM initiative.
3. Integrate ERM into the culture of the organization.
4. Focus on organization's top strategies and business objectives.
5. Identify key risks that could impair organization's objectives and relate to key strategies.
6. Start ERM initiatives with simple actions and build incrementally.
7. Leverage existing resources and risk management activities.

Practical Steps for Starting an ERM Initiative (continued)

Initial Action Steps

1. Seek board and senior management involvement and oversight.
2. Identify and position leader to drive ERM initiative.
3. Establish management working group:
   - To facilitate ERM initiative and support ERM leader
4. Inventory organization's existing risk management practices.
   - Perform analysis to reveal different approaches and ways to discuss risk across units.
5. Assess key strategies and related strategic risks.
   - "Black swans" or "unthinkable risks," i.e., low-frequency, high-impact events
6. Develop consolidated action plan and communicate to board of directors and management.
7. Develop and enhance risk reporting.
8. Develop next phase of action plans and ongoing communication.

Practical Steps for Starting an ERM Initiative (continued)

Strategic Risk Assessment Process

1. Understand strategies of the organization.
2. Gather data and views of strategic risks.
3. Prepare preliminary strategic risk profile; identify risks (possibility that events will occur and affect achievement of goals).
4. Validate and finalize strategic risk profile.
5. Develop enterprise risk management action plans.
   - Identify and select risk responses, mitigation activities, and risk reporting.
6. Communicate strategic risk profile and action plans (to directors and executive management, line management, and risk control units).
7. Implement ERM action plans (ongoing; revise strategies and risk profile as needed).

Summary

The world business environment is increasingly risk focused; a challenging environment demands a structured approach.

INFORMATION TECHNOLOGY AND COMMUNICATIONS

Risks and Controls in Computer-Based Accounting Information Systems

Consistency—Computers process data the same way every time.

Timeliness—Electronic processing and updating is normally more efficient.

Analysis—Data can be accessed for analytical procedures more conveniently (with proper software).

Monitoring—Electronic controls can be monitored by the computer system itself.

Circumvention—Controls are difficult to circumvent when programmed properly, and exceptions are unlikely to be permitted.

Risks and Controls in Computer-Based Accounting Information Systems (continued)

Overreliance—Without clear output, IT systems are often assumed to be working when they are not.

Access—Destruction and alteration of large amounts of data are possible if unauthorized access occurs.

Changes in programs—Severe consequences without detection are possible if unauthorized program changes occur.

Failure to change—Programs are sometimes not updated for new laws, rules, or activities.

Manual intervention—Knowledgeable individuals can sometimes alter files by bypassing the appropriate programs.

Loss of data—Catastrophic data loss is possible if appropriate controls aren't in place.

The COBIT Model of IT Governance and Management

COBIT 5 is a framework for integrating IT with business strategy and governance. It incorporates the following five principles:

1. Meeting stakeholder needs
2. Covering the enterprise end-to-end
3. Applying a single integrated framework
4. Enabling a holistic approach
5. Separating governance from management

The COBIT Model of IT Governance and Management (continued)

COBIT 5 enablers include:

- Processes—an organized set of practices to achieve objectives
- Organizational structures—the key decision-making entities in an organization
- Culture, ethics, and behavior of individuals and the organization
- Principles, policies and frameworks
- Information produced and used by the enterprise
- Services, infrastructure, and applications
- People, skills, and competencies required for successful completion of activities and making accurate decisions

Organizational Continuity Planning and Disaster Recovery

Unanticipated interruptions are avoided through **contingency planning** that includes fault-tolerant systems and backup files. One approach to backup is the **grandfather-parent-child** procedure in which three generations of files are retained.

A contingency plan will include a **disaster recovery plan** to prepare for the possibility of fires, floods, earthquakes, or terrorist bombings. The plan should specify backup sites to be used for alternate processing.

- A **hot site** is a location that includes a computer system that is already configured similarly to the system regularly used by the company, allowing for immediate use.
- A **cold site** is a location where power and space are available allowing for the installation of processing equipment on short notice.

Controls over **computer facilities** should include locating the facility in a safe place, limiting access to appropriate employees, and maintaining insurance.

Passwords or other forms of identification should be used to limit **access to computer files**.

System Development and Implementation

A Seven-Step Process (PADDTIM)

1. **P**lanning
   a. Define system to be developed
   b. Determine project scope
   c. Develop project plan
2. **A**nalysis
   a. Meet with users and IS staff
   b. Conduct needs assessment of users
   c. Conduct gap analysis between needs and existing systems
3. **D**esign (technical blueprint of new system)
4. **D**evelopment: Build
   a. Platform
   b. Software

A Seven-Step Process (PADDTIM) (continued)

5. **T**esting
   a. Unit tests (pieces of code)
   b. System tests (Do units within a system integrate?)
   c. Integration testing (Do separate systems integrate?)
   d. User acceptance
6. **I**mplementation: several strategies
   a. Parallel implementation: run old and new
   b. Plunge: Stop old, use new
   c. Pilot
   d. Phased
7. **M**aintenance
   a. Monitor and support
      1) Training
      2) Help desk
      3) Process and policies for authorizing changes

Introduction to E-Business and E-Commerce

Electronic commerce using **electronic data interchange** or **EDI** adds to the complexity of auditing. EDI enables:

- Communication without the use of paper
- Electronic funds transfers and sales over the Internet
- Simplification of the recording process using scanning devices
- Sending information to trading partners as transactions occur

EDI transactions are formatted using strict standards that have been agreed to worldwide, often requiring companies to acquire translation software.

Risks of E-Commerce

Electronic commerce increases the risk of improper use of information. Controls might include:

- Data encryption
- Controls to prevent electronic eavesdropping

There is also the risk of improper distribution of transactions with information being electronically transmitted to an inappropriate company. Controls might include:

- Routing verification procedures
- Message acknowledgement procedures

The reduction in the paper audit trail associated with EDI creates special challenges to the auditor.

- Detection risk may not be sufficiently reduced through substantive testing
- Control risk must be reduced adequately to achieve an acceptable level of audit risk
- Controls must be built into the system to insure the validity of information captured

Introduction to Enterprise-Wide and Cloud-Based Systems

Enterprise-Wide or Enterprise Resource Planning (ERP) Systems—ERPs provide transaction processing, management support, and decision-making support in a single, integrated, organization-wide software package. Goals of ERP systems include:

- Global visibility by using a single database
- Cost reductions by combining many functions into one system
- Employee empowerment, which gives relevant data to employees who need it in a timely manner for their job
- Best Practices—ERP systems are patterned after the most successful businesses in their industry

Cloud-Based Systems and Storage—An organization's decision to deploy cloud-based systems should flow from its enterprise architecture plan, which should include consideration of an IT sourcing strategy.

- Cloud systems are also called **the cloud, cloud computing, cloud storage,** and **cloud services**. In cloud-based storage, a virtual data pool is created by contracting with a third-party data storage provider.

Introduction to Enterprise-Wide and Cloud-Based Systems (continued)

Benefits of a cloud-based system include:

- Universal access by anyone with internet access and with the appropriate authority.
- Cost reduction, as maintenance costs are reduced by eliminating multiple systems.
- Scalability, as cloud-based systems can grow with organizations.
- Outsourcing and economies of scale by outsourcing data storage and management to organizations that have the capabilities and competencies to manage those facilities.

Data Governance and Data Management

Business and Its Data

- Management/Governance—key enabler of business success
    - Goal is to convert "data lake" (unfiltered pool of big data) into "data warehouse" (structured/filtered data repository for solving business problems).

Reciprocal Relationships between Business Processes and Data

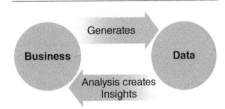

Source: Adapted from ISACA, 2020

Business and Its Data (continued)

Common Challenges

- Hard to quantify benefits
- Unclear assignment of data ownership
- Complying with increasing regulation of data ownership
- Changes in workflow impact enterprise systems and architectures
- Too much data (data deluge), disorganization, and data hoarding

Note: Data governance and management must be matched and mapped to an organization's strategy, market, structure and operations.

Two Phases and Five Stages of Data Governance and Management

- Phase 1: Design and Deploy—Covers Stages 1, 2, and 3
- Phase 2: Implement a Platform—Covers Stages 4 and 5
- Stage 1: Establish a data governance foundation (answers 4 questions: what data, when governance practice occurs, who is responsible, and how data is managed).

Two Phases and Five Stages of Data Governance and Management (continued)

- Stage 2: Establish/evolve data architecture.
- Stage 3: Define, execute, and ensure data quality, conduct data cleansing.
- Stage 4: "Democratize" data (i.e., create a single-source, searchable, curated database shared across the organization and available to all users).
- Stage 5: Focus on data analytics (primary purpose of data governance is to enable data analytics).

Data Governance Activities as Related to the Data Life Cycle

- The next exhibit illustrates the intersection of the data life cycle with data governance activities.

Data Governance Activities as Related to the Data Life Cycle (continued)

Mapping of Data Life Cycle to Data Governance Activities

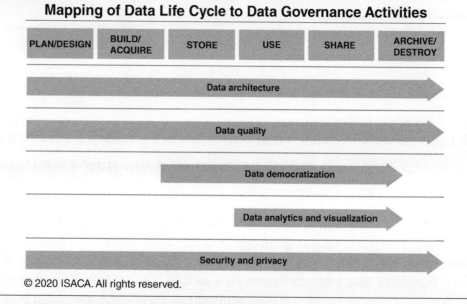

Focus on

Information Technology and Communications

64

Data Governance Structure and Data Stewardship Roles and Responsibilities

- **Data owners**—Strategic oversight role; responsible for data decisions and overall risk; quality, value, and utility of data
- **Data stewards**—Tactical role ensuring data assets are compliant and used. Also facilitates data consensus regarding data quality, use, and definitions.
- **Data custodians**—Operational role; ensure IT controls are operating/implemented. Manage IT architecture, implement IT capabilities.

Data Architecture—Three Levels of Standardizing Data Models

1. Conceptual—High level, abstract, enterprise-wide view
2. Logical—Adds detail to the conceptual level for more complete description of business requirements of data
3. Physical—Specifies how data will be encoded and stored in database (SQL and NoSQL). Considers processing, speed, accessibility, and distribution issues (cloud vs. local storage).

Good Data Governance Facilitates Data Analytics

1. Meaningful data analytics depend upon quality data that is reliable, relevant, and timely; the three data quality criteria are:

   - Intrinsic—Data values conform with actual, true values.
   - Contextual—Information is relevant and understandable to the task for which it is collected.
   - Security/accessibility—Controls are in place over availability and accessibility.

2. Through good data governance practices, the attributes necessary for high-quality data can be achieved.

3. Data governance is essential for creating quality, usable, and reusable data.

Data, Metadata, and Data Integrity

What Is Data?

- Data is a collection of facts and statistics brought together for reference or analysis.
- Data is found everywhere and is located in a variety of sources, including books, newspapers, data tables, photo archives, TV shows, movies, etc.
- Data is information about events, transactions, or entities that can be useful for decision-making purposes.
- Data set—A collection of data involving events that share common characteristics or relationships
- Data structures—Some data sets are highly structured (i.e., telephone books). Others are unstructured, with few rules to allow computer programs to parse (or divide up) the data based on those rules.

What Is Metadata?

- Metadata is information about data that helps to explain it; it extends and enhances data usefulness.
  1. Metadata increases the life of data by facilitating updates and revisions.
  2. Metadata increases data sharing and reuse and is essential for long-term data sets as assumptions/measures are likely to change over long time periods.
- Well-designed spreadsheets contain both data and metadata.

Three Criteria for Describing and Validating Data

1. The description includes the purpose of a data set.
    a. A data set's purpose/intended use is the most important element of metadata.
    b. Data may be collected for one specific purpose or for multiple, dissimilar purposes.
2. Description of data set is complete, accurate, and includes eight elements. (Use the acronym "PURPS STUFF," which refers to *p*opulation, *u*ncertainty, *r*ecords, *p*recision, *s*ample, *s*ources, *t*ime, *u*nits, *f*ields, and *f*ilters.)
3. The data description identifies information not included in the set but necessary to understand the data elements and data population.
    a. Example: Data that requires special knowledge to use or understand the data
    b. The provider of data should include this information in the data description.

Data, Metadata, and Data Integrity—Key Points

1. For data to be useful, the auditor/accountant must understand its quality/integrity.
2. Different data sets require different approaches to assess quality/integrity.
3. There are three important criteria to understand data integrity:
   a. Data's purpose
   b. Metadata's accuracy and completeness
   c. Identification of any missing information about the data set

Data Structures, Software, and Databases

Bit—A single switch in a computer that is either in the on (1) or off (0) position

Byte—A group of eight bits representing a character

Character—A letter, number, punctuation mark, or special character

Alphanumeric—A character that is either a letter or number

Field—A group of related characters representing a unit of information (such as a phone number or a city name)

File—A group of logically related records (such as the contact information for all employees)

- Master file—A permanent source that is used as an ongoing reference and that is periodically updated
- Detail file—A file listing a group of transactions that can be used to update a master file

Record—A group of logically related fields (such as the name, address, and telephone number of one employee)

Data Structures, Software, and Databases (continued)

Software is either system software or application software.

- **System software** is made up of the programs that run the system and direct its operations. It is comprised of the operating system and utility programs.
- **Utility** programs are used for sorts, merges, and other routine functions to maintain and improve the efficiency of a computer system.
- **Communication software** handles transmission of data between different computers.
- Specialized **security software** is a type of utility program used to control access to the computer or its files.

Programming languages:

- **Source program** is in the language written by the programmer (high-level languages resemble English while assembly languages are closer to direct machine instructions).
- **Object program** is in a form the machine understands (on-off or 1-0).
- **Compiler** is a program that converts source programs into machine language.

Information Systems Hardware

Hardware is the actual electronic equipment. Common components include:

- **Central processing unit** or **CPU**—The principal hardware component that processes programs
- **Memory**—The internal storage space or **online storage**, often referred to as **random access memory** or **RAM**
- **Offline storage**—Devices used to store data or programs externally, including floppy disks, magnetic tape, digital video discs (DVDs), and compact discs (CDs)
- **File server**—A computer with a large internal memory used to store programs and data that can be accessed by all workstations in the network
- **Input and output devices**—Devices that allow for communication between the computer and users and for the storage of data, such as a terminal with a screen and a keyboard, scanners, microphones, wireless handheld units, barcode readers, point-of-sale registers, optical character readers, mark sense readers, light guns, printers, speakers, CD and DVD drives, magnetic tape drives, and magnetic disk drives

Size and Power of Computers

Hardware comes in various sizes, depending on the volume and complexity of users' needs. In declining order of power, computer hardware includes:

- **Supercomputers**—Common for massive scale needs by science and math departments of universities and large governmental operations
- **Mainframe computers**—Until recently, often the only computer a large organization might have, with several terminals having the ability to connect to it simultaneously
- **Minicomputers**—Until recently, a less expensive alternative to mainframes used by smaller organizations as their primary computer with accessibility through multiple terminals
- **Microcomputers**—Personal computers designed for use by a single individual, including desktops and laptops
- **Personal digital assistants**—Handheld computers with limited processing capabilities that normally emphasize easy connection and transfer of data with the primary microcomputer used by an individual

Storage Devices

Magnetic tape—Inexpensive form of storage used primarily for backup, since only **sequential** access of data is possible.

Magnetic disks—Permanent storage devices inside a computer (including hard drives) that allow **random** access to data without the need to move forward or backward through all intervening data. Some systems use **RAID** (redundant array of independent disks), which includes multiple disks in one system so that data can be stored redundantly and the failure of one of the disks won't cause the loss of any data.

Removable disks—Transportable forms of storage. In increasing order of capacity, these include:

- Compact discs (CDs)
- Optical discs (DVDs)

Transaction Processing

The two primary approaches to the processing of data are batch processing and online processing.

1. **Batch processing**—Input data is collected over a period of time and processed periodically.
2. **Online processing**—Individuals originating transactions process them from remote locations in a batch, similar to batch processing, or immediately in an **online**, **real-time system**.

Online, real-time systems update accounting records immediately as transactions occur, but result in significant changes in internal control.

- Source documents are often not available to support input into the computer.
- The audit trail is usually significantly reduced, requiring controls programmed into the computer.

Accounting System Cycles

The accounting cycle is a way to categorize business and accounting activities. Many of these activities can be grouped into modules in a computerized accounting system. For example, different ERP systems group somewhat differing activities together into modules or cycles.

1. **Revenue cycle**—Interactions with customers (give goods; get cash)
2. **Expenditure cycle**—Interactions with suppliers (give cash; get goods)
3. **Production cycle**—Give labor and raw materials; get finished product
4. **Human resources/payroll cycle**—Hire, use, and develop labor; give cash and benefits
5. **General ledger, reporting, financing cycle**—Give cash; get cash; report financial outcomes

Emerging AIS Technologies

Emerging Payment Processing Systems

- Historically payment services were provided by financial institutions; they were very expensive to sellers.
- Emerging payment systems are simple to use, cheaper, and seller and user friendly. They reduce costs and increase online sales.
- Example payment systems
  - Credit cards
  - Apple Pay
  - Samsung Pay
  - Walmart Pay
  - PayPal
  - Venmo
  - Amazon "One-Click" payments

Internet of Things

- The Internet of Things (IoT) is the widespread connection of electronic devices to the internet.
- Recent news reports suggest that hackers are increasingly targeting (i.e., hacking) IoT applications.

Example Applications of IoT

- **Medicine and agriculture**: Real-time data feeds that monitor the status and condition of any living organism (e.g., Fitbit)
- **Insurance**: Sensory data on road conditions, weather, traffic, driver behavior, etc.
- **Banking**: Monitor use and status of ATMs, physical security of offices and buildings
- **Marketing**: Respond in real time to customers' interests and physical proximity

Internet of Things (continued)

Accounting Implications

- Automated information collection and data streaming for audits (internal and external) and tax engagements
- Real-time managerial accounting monitoring data
- New skill sets for CPAs: Managing the IoT and the resulting big data

Risks

- Privacy, intrusive devices: Detailed, personal data will become available about individuals and their behavior (e.g., medical and financial data)
- Complexities of data ownership, availability, distribution, storage
- The creation and management of big data

Automated IT Security: Authentication

Goal for User Authentication

Fully integrated, multifactor security, automated systems

1. The adoption of the IoT will lead to increasing use of automated security systems.
2. Authentication in these systems will use multiple identifiers. Identifiers may include:
   - Biometrics (e.g., fingerprints, iris scans, body scans, facial recognition)
   - Advanced analytics that identify system use patterns (e.g., typical login times, pressure and force on keyboard and mouse)
   - Objects (e.g., cellphones, key cards)

Risks and Prognosis

- Risks include the inevitable failures and shake-outs as vendors and users experiment with new authentication systems.
- Gartner Reports expects increasing waves of IT security automation that, in 10 to 20 years, will result in the *complete automation* of integrated, multifactor authentication systems.

Gamification

Gamification is the application of video gaming principles in simulations, or the use of badges and points as motivators, to engage users in learning content that is essential for their jobs.

What Is the Value of Gamification?

Gamification "makes learning fun again." It uses psychological principles based in graphics, design, images, motivation, and narrative (stories) to simulate actual scenarios that are relevant to users' jobs.

Example of Gamification

Some CPA firms use gamification to reward employees for engaging in health and wellness activities. By earning points for healthy, stress-reducing behaviors, employees not only take better care of themselves but also win prizes and rewards.

What Is Big Data?

Big data is the creation, analysis, storage, and dissemination of extremely large datasets.

Gartner Consulting Definition (paraphrased)

High volume, velocity, and/or a variety of information assets that demand new, innovative forms of processing for enhanced decision making, business insights or process optimization.

Sources of big data: Ubiquitous computing (i.e., smartphones and wearables, e.g., the Fitbit), the Internet of Things, and advances in biometrics (i.e., automated human recognition) are all sources for big data.

Governance: Organizations must establish a clear governance structure for big-data projects.

Another name for big data is "smart data," which generally refers to both big data and the use of advanced analytic methods on the data.

Value and Risks of Big Data

Some value/uses and risks of big data are listed below.

Value/Uses

- Marketing and sales
- Operational and financial performance
- Risk and compliance management
- Product and service innovation
- Improving customer experiences and loyalty
- Data monetization (sales)

Risks

- Privacy
- Legal issues and prohibited uses (e.g., of medical data and HIPPA)
- Technology and structure—Where and how will the data be stored and protected?

Bitcoin and Blockchain

What Is Bitcoin?

- Bitcoin is an intangible asset that can be bought, sold, and traded (in contrast, e.g., to goodwill).
- Bitcoin is also "electronic cash" (but is taxed as property not currency).
- Bitcoin is a decentralized currency that is not under the control of a centralized authority.
- Bitcoin is a network, payment, and accounting system.

Bitcoin Technology

- Bitcoins are created by "mining," which is solving mathematical puzzles requiring fast computers.
- The network: Accounting for (i.e., tracking) bitcoins operates on a **peer-to-peer network**.

What Is Bitcoin? (continued)

Bitcoin Risks

- New investments, including new currencies, have a heightened risk of fraud. Bitcoin investors and users may be targets for fraudsters and criminals.
- Do not expect to recover bitcoin losses from fraud.
- Holding and investing in bitcoins has unique risks.

What Is Blockchain?

- Blockchain is a decentralized, distributed ledger.
- Blockchain was created as part of the invention of bitcoins.
- A blockchain record is an electronic file that consists of "blocks," which document transactions.
- Because blockchain relies on decentralized users confirming one another's ledgers, it requires adoption by many users to be useful.

Blockchain Security

Blockchain security depends on three factors:

1. Independent confirmation
2. Asymmetric encryption
3. Cheap, fast computing capacity

What Is Blockchain? *(continued)*

Blockchain Applications

- Smart contracts
- Internet of Things
- Open source payments
- Corporate governance and financial reporting
- Predictive analytics
- Identity (i.e., authenticating user identities) and access management
- Auditing and monitoring

Risks and Limitations

- Hacks, cracks, and attacks

Blockchain technology is very complex and relies on sophisticated, advanced encryption and networking technologies.

Artificial Intelligence and Machine Learning

What Is Artificial Intelligence?

1. **Artificial intelligence (AI) is the creation of intelligent hardware and software.**
    - Most AI systems harvest and use big data. Example: machine learning systems are of little value without massive datasets to learn from.

2. **Categories of AI**
    - Machine learning (analysis)—These are systems that use big data to learn rules and categories to enable prediction and classification. Example: neural networks. A common accounting application: classifying journal entries.

What Is Artificial Intelligence? (continued)

- Robotics (activity)—Examples of robotic applications include machine-directed welding, controlling production, manufacturing, and distribution processes.
- Intelligent agents (engagement)—Computer "agents" that perform tasks, e.g., data harvesting and cleaning. Analysis of market trends, e.g., in purchasing airline tickets. Interact with humans (e.g., SIRI on the Apple iPhone)
- Expert systems (analysis and activity)—Expert systems build and apply expertise in a domain. May include machine learning or intelligent agent subsystems.

Levels of Intelligence

1. **Data Harvesting and Cleaning (lowest)**
   - Includes acquiring or extracting data (e.g., pulling it from databases or websites), cleaning (e.g., putting it in usable form), and validating data (confirming its accuracy).

2. **Analyzing Numbers**
   - Includes common financial and nonfinancial data analysis

3. **Analyzing Words, Images, and Sounds**
   - Includes the analysis of natural language disclosures in financial statements (e.g., 10-K SEC filings) and from audio files of conference calls

4. **Performing Digital Tasks**
   - Includes business process reengineering to improve efficiency and effectiveness

Levels of Intelligence (continued)

5. **Performing Physical Tasks**
   - Includes applications of robotics and drones, which include both physical devices and Internet of Things sensing and reporting technologies

6. **Self-Aware AI**
   - Does not exist and likely will not exist for 20 to 100 years. Such systems would rival (and eventually exceed?) human intelligence.

AI Benefits and Risks

AI Benefits

- Speed, accuracy, and cost
- Ability to scale up and speed up applications and to reduce costs

Short-Term Risks of Implementing AI

AI systems often include the biases of their developers. These can include:

- Data biases—Harvesting and creating datasets that omit relevant variables and considerations will create biased data sources.
- Prediction biases—Systems that include biased data will, obviously, generate biased predictions.
- Learned (or "emergent" or "confirmation") biases—Smart machines will learn and integrate the biases of those who train them.

AI Benefits and Risks (continued)

Medium-Term Risks of Implementing AI

- Lost jobs and disappearing employment—Some economists and computer scientists argue that many jobs will be lost to AI. Others argue that many jobs will be displaced but not lost.

- Legal and ethical issues—Who is liable when the AI screws up?

Summary and Conclusion

- AI and smart machines will change the nature of accounting work over the next 20 years. Opportunities exist within this disruption for accountants to partner with the machines to better serve clients and the public interest.
- Benefits from AI include scalability, improved service, accuracy (e.g., of predictions), and reduced costs.
- Risks of AI include bias, employment disruption, and unresolved legal, ethical, and privacy issues.

Computer Networks and Data Communications

In a computer network, computers are connected to one another to enable sharing of peripheral devices, sharing data and programs stored on a **file server**, and communicating with one another.

Networks allow various user departments to share information files maintained in **databases**. Databases should:

- Provide departments with information that is appropriate
- Prevent access to inappropriate information

A company may create its own **value-added network** or **VAN**.

- A **local area network** (**LAN**) is used when computers are physically near to one another
- A **wide area network** (**WAN**) uses high-speed, long-distance communications networks or satellites to connect computers that are not near to one another

Cloud computing is the use and access of multiple server-based computational resources via a digital network (WAN, Internet connection using the World Wide Web, etc.)

Computer Networks and Data Communications (continued)

To minimize control risk, a network should have some form of security that limits access to certain files to authorized individuals.

- Certain individuals may have read-only access to files
- Others will be authorized to alter the data in the files

A **virus** is a program that requests for a computer to perform an activity that is not authorized by the user. A **worm** is a program that duplicates itself over a network so as to infect many computers with viruses.

A tool for establishing security is a **firewall**, which prevents unauthorized users from accessing data.

The Internet—Structure and Protocols

The **Internet** is a worldwide network that allows virtually any computer system to link to it by way of an electronic gateway. The Internet facilitates data communication services including:

- Remote login
- File transfer
- Electronic mail
- Newsgroups
- Videoconferencing
- Groupware systems

Intranets use Internet technology in closed networks.

Extranets use Internet technology to link businesses with suppliers, customers, and others.

Networks are part of a decentralized processing system applying **distributed data processing**. Users share programs, peripheral devices, and data.

In **client/server computing**, smaller programs are distributed to the workstations, enabling the user to communicate with the network. This is referred to as front-end processing.

In **end user computing**, a user department generates and uses its own information.

The Internet—Structure and Protocols (continued)

To make the Internet more user-friendly, a framework for accessing documents was developed, known as the World Wide Web

- **Hypertext Transfer Protocol (HTTP)**—The language commonly understood by different computers to communicate via the Internet
- **Document**—A single file on any computer that is accessible through the Internet
- **Page**—The display that results from connection to a particular document on the Internet
- **Uniform Resource Locator (URL)**—The "address" of a particular page on the Internet
- **Web browser**—A program that allows a computer with a particular form of operating software to access the Internet and that translates documents for proper display
- **Server**—The computer that is "sending" the pages for display on another computer
- **Client**—The computer that is "receiving" the pages and seeing the display
- **Upload**—Sending information from a client to a server computer
- **Download**—Sending information from a server to a client computer

The Internet—Structure and Protocols (continued)

Web 2.0 is a second generation of the web. Refers to the era of web-based collaboration and community generated content via web-based software tools such as:

- **Blog**—An asynchronous discussion, or web log, led by a moderator that typically focuses on a single topic
- **Wiki**—An information-gathering and knowledge-sharing website that is developed collaboratively by a community or group
- **Twitter**—A micro-variation of a blog. Restricts input (tweets) to 140 characters

Many companies use software to monitor and manage their reputations in social media.

ECONOMIC CONCEPTS

Demand

As the price of a product increases, the quantity demanded by buyers decreases. This is reflected by a demand curve that is plotted with quantity demands on the x-axis (horizontal) and price on the y-axis (vertical):

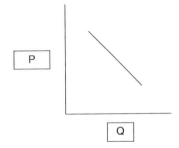

Demand Curve Shifts

When some variables other than the price of the product causes demand to change, it is referred to as a **demand curve shift.**

Positive shift—An increase in demand at each price (the line moves to the right)

Negative shift—A decrease in demand at each price (the line moves to the left)

Below is an illustration of a positive demand curve shift:

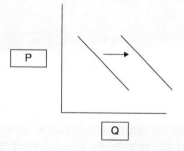

Positive Demand Curve Shift

Certain factors have a **direct** relationship to the demand curve for a product (an increase in that factor will cause the demand curve to have a positive shift to the right):

- **The price of substitute goods**—When another product may be an acceptable alternative, an increase in its price will make the present product more attractive. For example, an increase in the price of hamburgers will cause a positive shift in the demand for hot dogs.
- **Expectations of price increases**—Consumers are more likely to buy now if they think prices will be going up in the future.
- **Consumer income and wealth**—For **normal goods**, the demand will increase if consumers have more wealth to spend on goods.
- **Size of the market**—When new consumers are available to purchase a product, such as when trade barriers between countries are removed, demand for the product will increase.

Negative Demand Curve Shift

Certain factors have an **inverse** relationship to the demand curve for a product (an increase in that factor will cause the demand curve to have a negative shift to the left):

- **The price of complementary goods**—When products are normally used together, an increase in the price of one of the goods harms demand for the other. For example, an increase in the price of hamburgers will cause a negative shift in the demand for hamburger buns.

- **Consumer income and wealth**—For **inferior goods**, the demand will decrease if consumers have more wealth to spend on goods. For example, the demand for tire patches will likely decrease as people become wealthier, since they are more likely to be able to replace the tires rather than patch them.

- **Group boycott**—An organized boycott will, if effective, decrease the demand for a product.

Other factors affect the demand curve in significant but indeterminate ways, such as changes in consumer tastes.

Supply

As the price of a product increases, the quantity offered by sellers increases. This is reflected by a supply curve that is plotted with quantity on the x-axis (horizontal) and price on the y-axis (vertical):

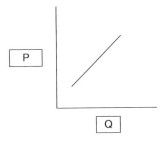

Supply Curve Shifts

When some variable other than the price of the product causes supply to change, it is referred to as a **supply curve shift.**

Positive shift—An increase in supply at each price (the line moves to the right)

Negative shift—A decrease in supply at each price (the line moves to the left)

This is an illustration of a positive supply curve shift:

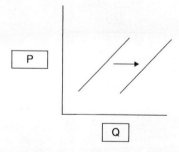

Factors Causing a Supply Curve Shift

Factors with a **direct** relationship on the supply curve include:

- Number of producers
- Government subsidies
- Price expectations

Factors with an **inverse** relationship on the supply curve include:

- Changes in production costs
- Prices of other goods

Market Equilibrium

The price at which the quantity demanded and quantity offered intersect is the equilibrium price:

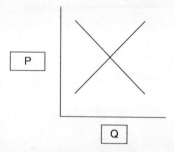

When the government intervenes to impose price ceilings, setting the price below equilibrium, the quantity demanded will exceed quantity offered, resulting in shortages of goods. When the government intervenes to impose price floors, setting price above equilibrium, the quantity offered will exceed quantity demanded, resulting in unsold surpluses of goods.

Focus on
Economic Concepts

Elasticity

Price Elasticity = Percentage change in quantity demanded / Percentage change in price

If elasticity is greater than 1, demand is considered **elastic**, and total revenue will decline if the price is increased, since the percentage drop in demand exceeds the percentage increase in price. A firm will be unable to pass on cost increases to consumers in these circumstances.

If elasticity is equal to 1, demand is considered **unitary**, and total revenue will remain the same if the price is increased.

If elasticity is less than 1, demand is considered **inelastic**, and total revenue will increase if the price is increased, since the percentage increase in price exceeds the decrease in demand. A firm will be able to raise prices in these circumstances.

Income Elasticity = Percentage change in quantity demanded / Percentage change in income

This will be a positive number for normal goods and a negative number for inferior goods.

Cross-Elasticity = Percentage change in demand for product X / Percentage change in price of product Y

This will be a positive number for substitute goods and a negative number for complements.

Consumer Demand and Utility Theory

Marginal utility—The satisfaction value to consumers of the next dollar they spend on a particular product.

Law of diminishing marginal utility—The more a consumer has of a particular product, the less valuable will be the next unit of that product. As a result, a consumer maximizes satisfaction when the last dollar spent on each product generates the exact same amount of marginal utility.

Personal disposable income—The available income of a consumer after subtracting payment of taxes or adding receipt of government benefits. The consumer will either spend (consume) or save this income.

Marginal propensity to consume (MPC)—The percentage of the next dollar in personal disposable income that the consumer would be expected to spend.

Marginal propensity to save (MPS)—The percentage of the next dollar in personal disposable income that the consumer would be expected to save (MPC plus MPS must equal 100%, or 1).

Inputs and the Cost of Production

Short-Run Costs of Production

Over short periods of time and limited ranges of production, costs include **fixed** and **variable** components:

Fixed costs—Costs that won't change even when there is a change in production. Average fixed costs are total fixed costs divided by units produced. An example is rent paid on the production facility.

Variable costs—Costs that will rise as production rises. Average variable costs are total variable costs divided by units produced. An example is materials used in the manufacture of the product.

Total costs—The sum of fixed and variable costs. Average total costs are total costs divided by units produced.

Marginal cost—The increase in cost that will result from an increase in one unit of production. Only variable costs are relevant, since fixed costs won't increase in such circumstances.

Long-Run Costs of Production

In the long run, all costs are variable, since increasing production beyond certain levels will require increases in capacity, causing even "fixed" costs to rise.

Return to scale is the increase in units produced (output) that results from an increase in production costs (input).

Return to scale = Percentage increase in output / Percentage increase in input

When return to scale is greater than 1, we have **increasing returns to scale**. This will normally occur up to a certain level for all firms because of **economies of scale**, or the increased efficiency that results from producing more units of a product (such as the ability to have employees specialize in different tasks and improve their abilities).

When return to scale is less than 1, we have **decreasing returns to scale**. This will normally occur beyond a certain level for all firms because of **diseconomies of scale**, or the increased inefficiencies that result from expanding production (such as the greater difficulty management has in controlling the activities of larger numbers of employees and facilities).

Firms should not increase production beyond levels at which marginal revenue from output exceeds marginal costs from inputs.

Gross Measures—Economic Activity

Gross domestic product (GDP)—The price of all goods and services produced by a domestic economy for a year at current market prices.

Real GDP—GDP adjusted to remove the effect of price inflation in the goods and services. In theory, real GDP growth above a certain level (called **potential GDP**) results in price inflation.

Gross national product (GNP)—The price of all goods and services produced by labor and property supplied by the nation's residents. It differs from GDP in two ways:

1. GNP includes income received by the nation's residents from other countries for products that are a part of foreign economies.
2. GNP excludes payments made to the residents of other countries for products that are a part of the domestic economy.

GDP/GNP may be computed using one of two different approaches:

1. **Income approach**—National income plus depreciation (and a few small adjustments)
2. **Expenditure approach**—Consumption plus private investment plus government purchases (and a few small adjustments)

Gross Measures—Employment/Unemployment

The unemployment rate is the percentage of those people who are looking for work who are currently not employed. There are three types of unemployment:

1. **Frictional**—This represents the time period during which people are unemployed because of changing jobs or newly entering the workforce. Because of the mobility of society, there is always some level of this type of unemployment, even in a society that effectively has "full" employment.

2. **Structural**—This represents potential workers whose job skills do not match the needs of the workforce because of changing demand for goods and services or technological advances that reduce or eliminate the need for the skills they possess. Such unemployment normally requires retraining for these individuals to be employable again.

3. **Cyclical**—This represents the unemployment caused by variations in the business cycle, when real GDP fails to grow at the pace necessary to employ all willing workers.

Aggregate Demand and Supply

Effects of Price Inflation

Just as there are demand and supply curves for individual products, aggregate curves can be depicted for overall prices and production of goods and services of an entire economy. Price inflation will shift the aggregate demand curve for several reasons:

- **Interest rate effect**—Price inflation causes an increase in interest rates and decreases the willingness of consumers to borrow, causing a negative shift in the demand curve for items whose purchase is typically financed, such as houses and automobiles.
- **Wealth effect**—Price inflation causes the value of fixed income investments (such as bonds) to decrease, causing individuals to have less wealth and reducing their consumption of normal goods. (The consumption of inferior goods will increase, but these are typically a small part of the overall economy.)
- **International purchasing power effect**—Domestic price inflation makes domestic goods and services more expensive relative to foreign goods and services, causing an increased demand for foreign products and a negative shift in the demand curve for domestic goods and services.

Business Cycle

Expansion—Periods of increased aggregate spending will cause a positive shift in the demand curve to the right and result in a higher equilibrium GDP. Technological advances will cause a positive shift in the supply curve and also result in a higher equilibrium GDP.

Contraction—Periods of decreased aggregate spending will shift the demand curve to the left and result in a lower equilibrium GDP. Trade wars between nations (and wars in general) cause a negative shift in the supply curve and also cause a decline in GDP.

Recession—Two consecutive quarters of negative GDP growth.

Depression—A contraction of GDP that continues for a long period of time. (There is no formal agreement as to the length of time a recession must continue to be called a depression, but it will usually be multiple years.)

Panic—A severe contraction of GDP occurring within a very short time frame (generally lasting less than a year).

Recovery—The term used to refer to the period of expansion that follows the end of a contraction.

Indicators of Business Cycles

Leading indicator—A measure that is used to try to predict recoveries and recessions. These indicators will normally start moving months before an actual recovery begins and start moving down months before an actual recession begins. There are many such indicators with variable success in predicting the business cycle. One of the most useful is changes in **stock market prices**.

Coincident indicator—A measure that normally moves up and down simultaneously with economic recoveries and recessions, respectively, and is used to determine if the economy is expanding or contracting at the present time. One example is **industrial production**.

Lagging indicator—A measure that normally starts moving up months after a recovery has begun and starts declining months after a recession has begun. It is used to confirm evidence that the economy has been expanding or contracting over the past few months. A commonly used lagging indicator is the **average prime rate** for bank loans.

Price Levels and Inflation/Deflation

There are three common measures of price inflation:

1. **Consumer price index (CPI)**—This measures the price of a fixed basket of goods and services that a typical urban consumer might purchase in relation to the price of the same goods and services in an earlier base period.
2. **Producer price index (PPI)**—This measures a fixed basket of goods at the wholesale cost to dealers (such as retail stores) rather than the price to consumers.
3. **GDP deflator**—This utilizes the total production of the economy as measured by GDP and is used to convert GDP to real GDP.

A decline in general price levels is known as **deflation**.

Demand-Pull Inflation

When aggregate spending increases, the **demand** curve moves to the **right**, causing the market equilibrium to occur at higher price levels:

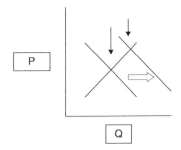

Notice that the equilibrium point occurs at a higher level of prices AND quantity. This is the basis for the historical theory that higher inflation results in higher productivity and, therefore, lower unemployment. The trade-off between inflation and unemployment is known as the **Phillips curve**. Many modern economists reject this theory, or believe that increases in inflation cause only a temporary decline in unemployment.

Cost-Push Inflation

When production costs increase, the **supply** curve moves to the **left**, causing the market equilibrium to occur at higher price levels:

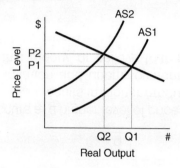

Notice that the equilibrium occurs at a higher level of prices but at a lower quantity. This means that prices are rising but output is declining, usually resulting in higher unemployment. This effect directly contradicts the theory of the Phillips curve.

Money, Banking, and Monetary/Fiscal Policy

There will be a positive shift in the demand curve when there is an increase in spending by consumers, businesses, or governments. The size of the shift will be significantly larger than the amount spent, due to the **multiplier effect** of increased spending increasing the income of suppliers, who in turn will spend more, increasing the income of other suppliers, and so on.

The size of the multiplier effect depends on the percentage of increased income that is expected to be spent, or the **marginal propensity to consume,** and the related percentage of increased income that is expected to be saved, or the **marginal propensity to save**. (These two must add up to 1 for the overall economy just as they did for each individual consumer.)

The increase in the equilibrium GDP that results from an injection of new spending is:

Change in spending / Marginal propensity to save

For example, if those making up the economy overall are likely to spend 75% of increased income and save the other 25%, then a change in spending of $100 will raise GDP by $400:

$$\$100 / 25\% = \$400$$

Focus on

Economic Concepts

121

Money, Banking, and Monetary/Fiscal Policy (continued)

Fiscal policy—By the way it collects taxes and spends, the government may try to aid certain industries or the economy as a whole. A common technique is known as **fiscal expansion** or **deficit spending**, which involves raising spending levels without an equivalent increase in taxes or lowering taxes without an equivalent decrease in spending. The goal is to increase aggregate spending in the economy and benefit from the multiplier effect.

Monetary policy—The Federal Reserve System (or "Fed") is charged with control over the money supply. By taking actions that increase (known as expansionary policies) or decrease (known as contractionary policies) the total amount of money in circulation, the Fed has a major impact on total spending. It has various techniques at its disposal:

- **Reserve requirements**—The Fed sets requirements on banks as to the percentage of checking deposit money received from customers that may not be loaned out.
- **Open-market operations**—The Fed can buy or sell government securities on the open market and thereby increase or decrease the money supply outstanding.
- **Discount rate**—The Fed can change the cost of money to banks and thereby cause a change in interest rates throughout the economy.

Reasons for International Activity

Because of differences in resources, climate, and specific skills, countries that trade goods and services with each other normally raise the standard of living of the people in both nations. Each country will focus on its advantages:

- **Absolute advantage**—This exists when the country can produce the goods at a lower cost than the other country.
- **Comparative advantage**—This exists when the cost of producing those goods relative to the cost of producing other goods is lower in that country than in the other country.

Even if one country has an absolute advantage over the other with respect to all goods, there will be trade benefits to both from each focusing on its comparative advantage. (On an individual level, a skilled CPA who is able to type 80 words per minute would still benefit from having word processing performed by a secretary who can type only 40 words per minute and who has no accounting skills.)

Obstacles to Free Trade

Free trade is restricted by **tariffs** (taxes on the importing of goods) and quotas (limits on the quantity that may be imported). When restrictions are imposed, their **direct** effects are:

- *Domestic producers: Positive.* Their demand curve shifts to the right as the availability of substitute goods has been reduced. They sell more goods at higher prices. Usually the managements and unions of these producers sought the restrictions.
- *Domestic users: Negative.* Their supply curve is being shifted to the left. As a result, they end up paying higher prices and acquiring fewer goods overall.
- *Foreign producers: Negative.* Their demand curve shifts to the left because the number of potential buyers has been reduced. They sell fewer goods at lower prices.
- *Foreign users: Positive.* Their supply curve shifts to the right, as their producers will have to do more selling in their own market. They buy more goods at lower prices.

A crucial **indirect** effect of trade restrictions is retaliation by other countries. The **World Trade Organization (WTO)** was formed to encourage all countries to maintain free trade policies and to prevent trade wars. The **North American Free Trade Agreement (NAFTA)** was signed by the United States, Mexico, and Canada to remove trade restrictions existing between these countries.

Balance of Payments

This is an account summary of the transactions of a nation with others.

Current account—The flow of goods and services and government transfers during a specific period:

- **Balance of trade**—The difference between the goods exported and goods imported. If exports are higher, then a trade surplus exists; if imports are higher, a trade deficit exists.
- **Balance of goods and services**—The same comparison, but with services included

Capital account—The flow of investments in fixed and financial assets

Balance of payments—The combined surplus or deficit from the current and capital accounts

Official reserve account—The total of gold and foreign currency held by the nation

Currency Exchange Rate Issue

The value of the currencies of different nations will fluctuate relative to one another based on the supply and demand for these currencies. Exchange rates between currencies include:

- **Spot rate**—The exchange rate for currencies that will be immediately delivered.
- **Forward rate**—The rate at which two parties agree they will exchange the currencies at a specific future date (called the settlement date).

Forward rates differ from spot rates based on expectations that the relative values of the two currencies will change between now and then. Factors affecting foreign exchange rates:

- **Inflation**—The currency with higher inflation will fall in value relative to the other.
- **Interest rates**—The currency in the nation with higher interest rates will rise in value.
- **Balance of payments**—The currency of the country that is a net exporter will rise in value.
- **Government intervention**—The currency will rise if official reserves are used to buy it.
- **Political and economic stability**—The currency will fall when there are threats to stability.

Introduction to Business Strategy and Market Analysis

Strategic planning involves identifying an organization's long-term goals and determining the best approaches to achieving those goals.

- Develop mission
- Develop vision
- Perform situational analysis to identify internal and external forces that may affect the organization's performance and choice of strategies and assess the organization's strengths, weaknesses, opportunities, and threats (a SWOT analysis)

Generic Strategies

- Product differentiation
- Cost leadership

FINANCIAL MANAGEMENT

Introduction to Financial Management

Five functions:

1. **Financing**—Raising capital to fund the business
2. **Capital budgeting**—Selecting the best long-term projects based on risk and return
3. **Financial management**—Managing cash flow so that funds are available when needed at the lowest cost
4. **Corporate governance**—Ensuring behavior by managers that is ethical and in the best interests of shareholders
5. **Risk management**—Identifying and managing the firm's exposure to all types of risk

Leverage

Operating leverage—The degree to which a firm has built fixed costs into its operations

- Higher fixed costs mean more risk when revenues are below expectations
- Profit grows rapidly relative to revenue increases due to lower variable costs
- Percentage change in operating income / Percentage change in unit volume = Degree of operating leverage

Financial leverage—The degree to which a firm uses debt financing in its business

- Higher debt means higher interest and principal obligations for repayment, increasing risk if performance is not up to expectations
- Debt financing costs less than equity financing and doesn't increase with greater performance, so overall profit and asset growth potential is greater
- Percentage change in earnings per share / Percentage change in earnings before interest and taxes = Degree of financial leverage

Cost Concepts

Debt—The cost of debt financing is the after-tax cost of interest payments, as measured by the yield to maturity. It can be calculated in two ways:

1. Yield to maturity × (1 − Effective tax rate)
2. (Interest expense − Tax deduction for interest) / Carrying value of debt

Preferred stock—The cost of preferred stock financing is the stipulated dividend divided by the issue price of the stock.

Common stock—The cost of common stock financing represents the expected returns of the common shareholders and is difficult to estimate. Some techniques:

- **Capital asset pricing model (CAPM)**—Volatility of a stock price relative to average stock. This model assumes the expected return of a particular stock depends on its volatility (beta) relative to the overall stock market. CAPM = Beta × Excess of normal market return over risk-free investments + Normal return on risk-free investments

- **Arbitrage pricing model**—This model is a more sophisticated CAPM with separate excess returns and betas for each component making up the stock characteristics

Cost Concepts (continued)

- **Bond yield plus**—This uses the normal historical relationship between equities and debt and simply adds 3% to 5% to the interest rate on the firm's long-term debt
- **Dividend yield plus growth rate**—This takes the current dividend as a percentage of the stock price and adds the expected growth rate in earnings

Weighted-average cost of capital—This is a calculation of a firm's effective cost of capital, taking into account the portion of its capital that was obtained by debt, preferred stock, and common stock. For example, if 40% of capital was obtained through long-term debt at an effective cost of 6%, 10% of capital was obtained by issuing preferred stock with an effective cost of 8%, and 50% of capital was obtained by issuing common stock expected to return 11% to shareholders, the weighted-average cost of capital is:

$$40\% \times 6\% + 10\% \times 8\% + 50\% \times 11\%$$

$$= 2.4\% + 0.8\% + 5.5\%$$

$$= 8.7\%$$

Time Value of Money Tools

Many decisions require adjustments related to the time value of money:

- **Present value of amount**—This is used to examine a single cash flow that will occur at a future date and determine its equivalent value today.

- **Present value of ordinary annuity**—This refers to repeated cash flows on a systematic basis, with amounts being paid at the end of each period. (It may also be known as an annuity in arrears.) Bond interest payments are commonly made at the end of each period and use these factors.

- **Present value of annuity due**—This refers to repeated cash flows on a systematic basis, with amounts being paid at the beginning of each period. (It may also be known as an annuity in advance or special annuity.) Rent payments are commonly made at the beginning of each period and use these factors.

- **Future values**—These look at cash flows and project them to some future date, and include all three variations applicable to present values.

- **Interest rates**—Usually, two components:
  1. Expected inflation/deflation rates
  2. Inflation-adjusted return for the investment (risk adjusted)

Focus on

Financial Management

Interest Rate Concepts and Calculations

This term refers to the price that borrowers must pay for the use of money.

- **Nominal interest rate**—The rate as measured in terms of the nation's currency
- **Real interest rate**—The rate adjusted for inflation
- **Risk-free interest rate**—The rate that would be charged to a borrower if the lender had an absolute certainty of being repaid (the rate paid on United States Treasury securities is often considered to be a useful measure of the risk-free interest rate)
- **Discount rate**—The rate set by the Federal Reserve System at which a bank can borrow from a Federal Reserve bank
- **Prime rate**—The rate that banks charge their most creditworthy customers on short-term loans from the bank

Financial Valuation

Three major valuation models for financial instrument assets in order of reliability:

1. Market values from active markets for identical assets
   a. Assumes sufficient volume
   b. For business purposes, value is measured in money.
2. Active markets for similar assets
   a. Must adjust for differences in instruments, for example:
      1) Block sales
      2) Credit risks
      3) Maturity/exercise dates
3. Valuation models
   a. In absence of active markets, assume hypothetical seller/buyer
   b. Generally use discounted cash flow
   c. Must use assumptions that are reasonable and consistent with existing general market information

Introduction and the Payback Period Approach

Used to evaluate capital expenditures—uses two equations

        Cash inflows before tax

$-$ Depreciation on investment

$=$ Increase in taxable income

$-$ Tax

$=$ Increase in accounting net income

	Cash inflows before tax	**or**		Increase in accounting net income
$-$	Tax		$+$	Depreciation on investment
$=$	After-tax net cash inflows		$=$	After-tax net cash inflows

Focus on

Financial Management

135

Payback Method

     Initial investment

÷   After tax net cash inflows

=   Payback period

Payback period is compared to target period

- If shorter, investment is acceptable
- If longer, investment is unacceptable

Traditional payback method does not consider time value of money

Present value payback method considers the time value of money

Accounting Rate of Return Approach

        Increase in accounting net income

÷   Investment

=   Accounting rate of return

Investment may be

- Initial investment
- Long-term average – (Initial investment + Salvage value) / 2
- Short-term average – (Beginning carrying value + Ending carrying value) / 2

Return compared to target rate

- If greater, investment is acceptable
- If lower, investment is unacceptable

Accounting rate of return does not consider the time value of money

Net Present Value Approach

After-tax net cash inflows
$\times$ Present value factor for annuity at target rate
$=$ Present value of investment
$-$ Initial investment
$=$ Net present value

If positive, investment is acceptable—if negative, investment is unacceptable

Internal Rate of Return Approach

        Initial investment

$\div$ After-tax net cash inflows

$=$ Present value factor (same as payback period)

The present value factor is compared to factors for the same number of periods (life of investment) to determine the effective interest rate.

- Factor may be equal to amount at specific interest rate
- If factor falls between amounts, rate is estimated

Resulting rate compared to target rate

- If greater, investment is acceptable
- If lower, investment is unacceptable

Introduction and Financial/Capital Structure

Long-Term Debt

Private debt—Loans obtained from banks and other financial institutions or from syndicates of lenders. Virtually all such loans have variable interest rates that are tied to an index:

- **Prime rate**—This is the rate that the lender charges its most creditworthy customers. Loans to other customers would include a fixed amount above this (e.g., prime plus 2%).
- **London Interbank Offered Rate (LIBOR)**—When the borrower and lender are in different countries, the base used will typically be the LIBOR rather than the prime rate.

Public debt—To bypass institutional lenders, a corporation may sell bonds directly to investors as a means of borrowing, with fixed interest rates and maturity dates for the securities, which can then trade on the open market.

- **SEC registered bonds**—To be sold on U.S. markets, bonds must satisfy the stringent registration and disclosure requirements of the SEC.
- **Eurobonds**—Bonds denominated in U.S. dollars can be sold on the European exchanges, which have less stringent requirements.

Debt Covenants

Borrowers often must agree to obey restrictions, or debt covenants.

Positive covenants might include:

- Providing annual audited financial statements to the lender
- Maintaining minimum ratios of current assets to current liabilities or financial measures
- Maintaining life insurance policies on key officers or employees of the company

Negative covenants might include:

- Not borrowing additional sums during the contract period from other lenders
- Not selling certain assets of the business
- Not paying dividends to shareholders
- Not exceeding certain compensation limits for executives

Bonds

Debt obligations may be secured by certain collateral or may specifically be placed behind other forms of debt in the priority of repayment. In roughly declining order of safety (and increasing order of interest rate), there are:

- **Mortgage bonds**—Secured by certain real estate owned by the borrower
- **Collateral trust bonds**—Secured by financial assets of the firm
- **Debentures**—Unsecured bonds
- **Subordinated debentures**—Unsecured bonds that will be repaid after all other creditors in the event of a liquidation of the corporation
- **Income bonds**—Bonds whose interest payments will be made only out of earnings of the corporation

Provisions Affecting Repayment of Bonds

The repayment of bonds may be affected by various provisions:

- **Term bonds**—Principal will be repaid on a single maturity date.
- **Serial bonds**—Principal repayment will occur in installments.
- **Sinking funds**—Regular deposits will be made by the borrower into an account from which repayment of the bonds will be made.
- **Convertible bonds**—The bondholder may convert the bonds to the common stock of the company as a form of repayment instead of holding them to maturity for cash.
- **Redeemable bonds**—The bondholder may be able to demand repayment of the bonds in advance of the normal maturity date should certain events occur (such as the buyout of the company by another firm).
- **Callable bonds**—The borrowing firm may force the bondholders to redeem the bonds before their normal maturity date (usually there is a set premium above the normal redemption price to compensate them for this forced liquidation).

Bond Interest Rates

There are three interest rates relevant to bonds:

1. **Stated rate**—The fixed interest payment calculated from the face value of the bond. It is also known as the **coupon rate, face rate,** or **nominal rate.**

2. **Current yield**—The fixed interest payment divided by the current selling price of the bond. When the bond is trading at a discount, this rate will be higher than the stated rate, and when the bond is trading at a premium, this rate will be lower than the stated rate. This rate can be somewhat misleading, since it reports the interest payment as a percentage of the current price but doesn't consider the fact that the principal repayment of the bond will not be the current selling price but the face value.

3. **Yield to maturity**—The interest rate at which the present value of the cash flows of interest and principal will equal the current selling price of the bonds. For a bond selling at a discount, it will be even higher than the current yield, since it accounts for the "bonus" interest payment reflected in the discount. For a bond selling at a premium, this rate will be even lower than the current yield, since it reflects the loss of the premium when the principal is repaid. This rate is also known as the **effective rate** or **market rate.**

Variations on Bond Interest

Zero-coupon bond—This bond makes no interest payments at all and only pays the face value on the date of maturity. Short-term U.S. Treasury bills are a common example. A zero-coupon bond will always sell at a discount, since the interest is represented entirely by the difference between the price at which it is bought and the face value paid at maturity.

Floating rate bond—The interest payment is not fixed but fluctuates with some general index of interest rates. A **reverse floater** pays more interest when the general index goes down and less interest when the index goes up. Such an unusual bond might be used to hedge against the risk associated with floating rate bonds that the firm has issued.

Registered bond—The bondholder's name is registered with the firm, and interest payments are sent directly to the registered owner. In such cases, an actual bond certificate usually will not be issued.

Junk bond—This bond pays much higher than normal interest, since it was issued by a firm that has a poor credit rating and is more likely to default on its obligations. Bonds with a credit rating by Moody's Investors Service lower than Baa are usually considered junk bonds.

Foreign bond—This simply refers to a bond in which interest and principal is paid in another currency.

Preferred Stock

Preferred stock shareholders receive a stipulated dividend and priority over common shareholders in the event of liquidation of the business. Additional features of preferred stock may include:

- **Cumulative dividends**—If stipulated dividends are not declared in a specific year, the amount becomes dividends in arrears and must be paid in later years before the common shareholders can receive any distribution.
- **Redeemability**—The shareholders may demand repayment of the face value at a specific date. In some cases, redemption is automatic. Such shares more closely resemble debt and are often presented before equity in the balance sheet.
- **Callability**—The firm may force the shareholders to redeem the shares.
- **Convertibility**—Shareholders can convert these shares to common stock.
- **Participation**—Preferred shareholders will receive a dividend that is higher than the stipulated rate when the common shareholders receive a higher rate.
- **Floating rate**—The dividend is variable based on some interest or inflation index.

Common Stock

Common stock shareholders are entitled to the residual (or leftover) assets and income after all creditors and preferred shareholders are paid.

Advantages to firm:

- The firm has no specific obligation to pay investors, increasing financial flexibility.
- Increased equity reduces the risk to lenders and reduces borrowing costs.

Disadvantages to firm:

- Issuance costs are greater than for debt.
- Ownership and control must be shared with all the new shareholders.
- Dividends are not tax-deductible.
- Shareholders ultimately receive a much higher return than lenders if the business is successful, so the long-run cost of capital obtained this way is typically much higher.

Introduction to Working Capital Management

Inventory conversion period (ICP) or inventory conversion cycle (ICC)—The average number of days required to convert inventory to sales

- ICP (ICC) = Average inventory / Cost of sales per day
- Average inventory = (Beginning inventory + Ending inventory) / 2
- Assume 365 days in a year unless told otherwise

Accounts receivable cycle (ARC)—The average number of days required to collect accounts receivable

- ARC = Average receivables / Credit sales per day

Accounts payable cycle (APC)—The average number of days between the purchase of inventory on account (including materials and labor for a manufacturing entity) and payment for them

- APC = Average payables / Purchases per day

Cash conversion cycle (CCC)—The average number of days between the payment of cash to suppliers of material and labor and cash inflows from customers

- CCC = ICP + ARC – APC

Cash Management

Cash balances are maintained by a firm for:

- **Operations**—To pay ordinary expenses
- **Compensating balances**—To receive various bank services, fee waivers, and loans
- **Trade discounts**—Quick payment of bills for early payment discounts
- **Speculative balances**—Funds to take advantage of special business opportunities
- **Precautionary balances**—Amounts that may be needed in emergency situations

Float refers to the time it takes for checks to be mailed, processed, and reflected in accounts. Management techniques try to maximize float on payments and minimize it on receipts.

- **Zero-balance accounts**—The firm is notified each day of checks presented for payment and transfers only the funds needed to cover them.
- **Lockbox system**—Customers send payments directly to bank to speed up deposits.
- **Concentration banking**—Customers pay to local branches instead of main offices.
- **Electronic funds transfers**—Customers pay electronically for fastest processing.

Short-Term Securities Management

To maximize earnings on free cash, a firm may utilize various investments. Investments that are available through the federal government include:

- **Treasury bills**—Short-term obligations backed by the United States with original lives under 1 year that can be bought and sold easily from issuance to maturity date. These are in zero-coupon form and pay no formal interest, so they trade at a discount to maturity value.
- **Treasury notes**—Obligations with initial lives between 1 to 10 years. Formal interest payments are made semiannually.
- **Treasury bonds**—Same as notes but with original lives over 10 years
- **Treasury Inflation-Protected Securities (TIPS)**—Treasury notes and bonds that pay a fixed rate of interest but with principal adjusted semiannually for inflation
- **Federal agency securities**—Offerings that may or may not be backed by the full faith and credit of the United States and don't trade as actively as Treasuries but pay slightly higher rates

Short-Term Securities Management (continued)

Other possible investments with free cash include:

- **Certificates of deposit**—Time deposits at banks that have limited government insurance
- **Commercial paper**—Promissory notes from corporations with lives up to 9 months
- **Banker's acceptance**—A draft drawn on a bank but payable at a specific future date (not on demand, as checks would be), usually 30 to 90 days after being drawn. These are usually generated by corporations to pay for goods, and may trade in secondary markets prior to the due date for payment at a discount.
- **Money market fund**—Shares in a mutual fund that invests in instruments with an average maturity date under 90 days, and which generally maintains a stable value for investors
- **Short-term bond fund**—Shares in a mutual fund that invests in instruments with an average life over 90 days but under 5 years, generating higher returns than a money market fund but with some fluctuation in the principal value of the fund
- **Equity and debt securities**—Individual stocks and bonds with substantially higher potential returns but also greater risk, including the risk of default. Should consider purchasing credit default insurance.

Accounts Receivable Management

A company sets credit policies for the granting and monitoring of receivables, including:

- **Credit period**—The time allowed for payment (typically 30 days)
- **Discounts**—Percentage reduction for early payment (such as 2% for payment in 10 days)
- **Credit criteria**—Financial strength requirements for customer to be granted credit
- **Collection policy**—Methods used to collect slow-paying accounts

In utilizing receivables to generate immediate cash, a firm's receivables may be:

- **Pledged**—A type of loan that is obtained with the receivables offered as collateral for the loan
- **Factored**—The receivables are actually sold to a financing company, which accepts the risk of noncollection and charges a percentage fee for accepting that risk (based on an estimate of the uncollectible rate) as well as an interest rate based on the funds advanced prior to the date when collection of the receivables is due.

Quality and Inventory Management

Economic Order Quantity (EOQ)

Minimizes total of order cost and carrying cost:

- **Order cost**—Cost of placing an order or starting a production run
- **Carrying cost**—Cost of having inventory on hand

$$EOQ = \sqrt{2AP/S}$$

A = Annual demand in units
P = Cost of placing an order or beginning a production run (order cost)
S = Cost of carrying one unit in inventory for one period (carrying cost)

Reorder Point and Safety Stock

Reorder point

- Units in inventory when order should be placed
- Average daily demand × Average lead time = Reorder point

Safety stock

- Extra units in inventory when placing an order in case demand or lead time is greater than average
- Avoids costs associated with running out of stock
- Maximum daily demand × Maximum lead time – Reorder point = Safety stock

Just-in-Time (JIT) Purchasing

Costs reduced through:

- Reduction in inventory quantities
- Elimination of non-value-added operations
- Most appropriate when order cost is low and carrying cost is high

Requires high-quality control standards

- Efficient system minimizing defective units
- Corrections made as defects occur
- Fewer vendors and suppliers

Just-in-Time (JIT) Purchasing (continued)

Problems of JIT system:

- Difficult to find suppliers able to accommodate
- High shipping costs due to smaller orders
- Potential problems due to delays in deliveries

May use backflush approach

- All manufacturing costs charged to cost of goods sold (COGS)
- Costs allocated from COGS to inventories at reporting dates (i.e., recording the costs associated with producing goods or services after they are produced, completed, or sold)

Quality Control

ISO Quality Standards—A series of standards established by the International Organization of Standards.

- **ISO 9000 Series**—Standards consisting of five parts (9000 to 9004) that focus on the quality of products and services provided by firms
- **ISO 14000 Series**—Standards focused on pollution reduction and other environmental goals

Pareto Principle—An attempt to focus on the small number of significant quality issues, based on an estimate that 80% of all problems come from only 20% of all causes.

Six Sigma Quality—A statistical measure of the percentage of products that are in acceptable form, based on standard deviation measures. One sigma means that approximately 68% of products are acceptable. Six sigmas would indicate 99.999997% of products meet quality standards, and constitute a hypothetical goal of perfection in manufacturing.

Kaizen—Japanese art of continuous improvement. This theory emphasizes identification by all members of a company of small potential improvements rather than searching for big breakthroughs.

Delphi—Separate consultation with multiple experts and tabulation of recommendations.

Cost of Quality

The costs related to quality rise the later in the process the firm deals with it. There are four different stages at which costs can be addressed:

1. **Prevention costs**—Prevent product failure

   - Use high-quality materials
   - Inspect production process
   - Train employees
   - Maintain machines

2. **Appraisal or detection costs**—Detect product failure before production is complete

   - Inspect samples of finished goods
   - Obtain information from customers

Cost of Quality (continued)

3. **Internal failure costs**—Detect product failure after production but before shipment to customer

   - Scrap resulting from wasted materials
   - Reworking units to correct defects
   - Reinspection and retesting after rework

4. **External failure costs**—Defective product sent to customer

   - Warranty costs
   - Dealing with customer complaints
   - Product liability
   - Marketing to improve image
   - Lost sales

Liquidity Measures

Current Ratio = Current assets / Current liabilities

Quick (or Acid Test) Ratio = Quick assets / Current liabilities

- **Quick assets** = Cash and Cash equivalents + Short-term marketable securities + Accounts receivable (net) / Current liabilities

Operational Activity Measures

Receivable Turnover = Net credit sales / Average accounts receivable

- **Average Accounts Receivable (A/R)** = (Beginning A/R + Ending A/R) / 2
- Remember to use net credit sales, **not** net sales

Receivables Collection Period = Average accounts receivable / Average credit sales per day

- Use a 365-day year unless told otherwise

Inventory Turnover = Cost of goods sold / Average inventory

- Remember to use cost of goods sold, **not** sales

Inventory Conversion Period = Average inventory / Average cost of goods sold per day

Fixed Asset Turnover = Sales / Average net fixed assets

- Remember that net fixed assets are after subtraction of accumulated depreciation

Total Asset Turnover = Sales / Average total assets

Profitability Measures

Gross Profit Margin = Gross profit / Net sales

Gross Margin = Sales (net) − Cost of goods sold / Net sales

Operating Profit Margin = Operating profit / Net sales

Return on Assets = Net Income / Average Total Assets

Return on Total Assets = [Net income + (add back) Interest expense (net of tax effect)] / Average total assets

- **Average Total Assets** = (Beginning total assets + Ending total assets) / 2

Return on Equity = Net income / Average total equity

- **Average Stockholders' Equity** = (Beginning total equity + Ending total equity) / 2

Return on Common Stockholders' Equity = [Net income − Preferred dividend (obligation for the period only)] / Average common stockholders' equity

- **Average Common Stockholders' Equity** = (Beginning common stockholders' equity + Ending common stockholders' equity) / 2

Equity/Investment Leverage Measure

Debt to Total Assets = Total liabilities / Total assets

Debt to Equity Ratio = Total liabilities / Total equity

Times Interest Earned Ratio = Earnings before interest expense and taxes (EBIT) / Interest expense

Focus on
Financial Management

163

PERFORMANCE MEASURES AND MANAGEMENT TECHNIQUES

Manufacturing Costs

Cost Classifications

Product and Period Costs

	Product	Period
Direct materials (DM)	x	
Direct labor (DL)	x	
Manufacturing overhead (MOH)	x	
Selling, general, and administrative expenses (SG&A)		x

Cost Classifications (continued)

Prime and Conversion Costs

	Prime	Conversion
DM	X	
DL	X	X
MOH		X

Variable and Fixed Costs

	Variable	Fixed
DM	X	
DL	X	
MOH	X	X
SG&A	X	X

Costing Methods

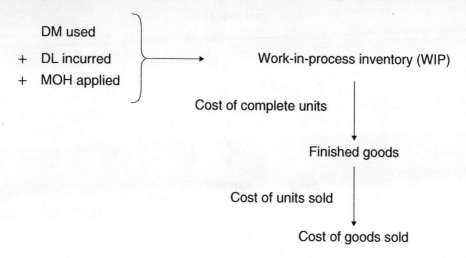

DM used
+ DL incurred
+ MOH applied

→ Work-in-process inventory (WIP)

Cost of complete units

↓

Finished goods

Cost of units sold

↓

Cost of goods sold

Manufacturing Overhead

1. Calculate the predetermined overhead rate (POHR)

   Estimated variable MOH for period

   +   Estimated fixed MOH for period

   =   Estimated total MOH for period

   ÷   Estimated # of units for period (cost driver)

   =   Predetermined overhead rate (POHR)—often split into fixed and variable rates

2. Apply MOH to WIP

        Actual # of units for period (cost driver)

   ×   POHR

   =   MOH Applied

Manufacturing Overhead (continued)

3. Determine under-applied or over-applied MOH
   - Actual MOH > MOH applied: MOH under applied
   - Actual MOH < MOH applied: MOH over applied
4. Dispose of under-applied or over-applied MOH
   - Generally added to or deducted from cost of goods sold (COGS)
   - May be charged or credited directly to income
   - May be allocated to WIP, finished goods, and COGS

Spoilage, Cost, and Inventory Flows

Different types of unused units or materials have different accounting treatments:

Normal spoilage—Product cost (added to cost of goods sold)

Abnormal spoilage—Period cost (charged against income in period)

Scrap—Generally charged to cost of goods manufactured

Proceeds from sale of scrap:

- Additional income
- Reduce cost of sales
- Reduce manufacturing overhead
- Reduce cost of specific job

Cost Behavior Patterns

Calculating Total Costs

Total costs = Fixed costs + Variable costs

$y = a + bx$

y = Total cost (dependent variable)

a = Total fixed costs

b = Variable cost per unit

x = # of units (independent variable)

Various methods are used to determine the variable cost per unit and total fixed costs

Cost Drivers

Units represent volume of cost driver

- Cost driver can be any variable that has greatest influence on cost
- Examples include volume of production, hours worked, miles driven, or machine hours

High-Low Method

Four steps in estimating variable cost per unit and total fixed costs

1. | | | |
   |---|---|---|
   | Highest volume | Total cost | # of units |
   | Lowest volume | Total cost | # of units |
   | Difference | Cost | # of units |

2. Variable cost per unit = Difference in cost ÷ Difference in # of units
3. Total variable costs (at either level) = Variable cost per unit × # of units
4. Fixed costs (at either level) = Total costs − Total variable costs

Regression Analysis

Coefficient of correlation (R) indicates relationship between dependent and independent variable:

- R = 1   Strong direct relationship
- 1 > R > 0   Direct relationship, not as strong
- R = 0   No relationship
- 0 > R > −1   Indirect relationship, not as strong
- R = −1   Strong indirect relationship

Company will use cost driver with strongest direct or indirect relationship

Activity-Based Costing and Process Management

Method of analyzing and reducing MOH

- MOH segregated into pools
- Cost driver identified for each pool
- MOH applied using multiple rates

Identifies costs that are non-value-added costs

- Can be used to reduce overhead
- Identify and minimize non-value-added costs

Also used to allocate service department costs

Under step allocation method

- Service departments allocated beginning with those serving most other departments
- Allocation based on that department's cost driver
- Costs allocated to all remaining service departments and production departments
- Costs not charged back to service departments already allocated
- Process complete when only production departments remain

Focus on

Performance Measures and Management Techniques

173

		Service departments				Production departments	
		#1	**#2**	**#3**	**#4**	**#1**	**#2**
Costs		$	$	$	$	$	$
	Allocation	($)	$	$	$	$	$
Subtotal		0	$	$	$	$	$
	Allocation		($)	$	$	$	$
Subtotal			0	$	$	$	$
	Allocation			($)	$	$	$
Subtotal				0	$	$	$
	Allocation				($)	$	$
Total					0	$	$

Absorption and Direct Costing

Absorption Costing

- Used for financial statements
- Inventory includes DM + DL + Variable MOH + Fixed MOH

Variable Costing

- Used for internal purposes only
- Inventory includes DM + DL + Variable MOH

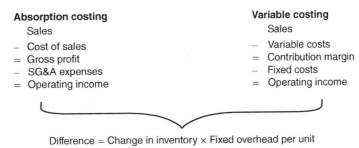

Absorption costing	Variable costing
Sales	Sales
– Cost of sales	– Variable costs
= Gross profit	= Contribution margin
– SG&A expenses	– Fixed costs
= Operating income	= Operating income

Difference = Change in inventory × Fixed overhead per unit

Job Order Costing and Overhead Allocation

Used when units are relatively expensive and costs can be identified to specific units or batches

- DM, DL, and MOH applied charged to WIP
- Cost of completed units removed from WIP and charged to finished goods
- Cost of units sold removed from finished goods and charged to COGS

Process Costing

Used when units are relatively inexpensive and costs cannot be identified to units or batches

- DM, DL, and MOH applied charged to WIP
- Calculates average cost of equivalent units produced during period
- Average costs used to transfer from WIP to finished goods and from finished goods to COGS

Calculating equivalent units

- Costs incurred at beginning of process—Equivalent units = Units × 100%
- Costs incurred at end of process—Equivalent units = Units × 0%
- Costs incurred uniformly—Equivalent units = Units × % complete
- Costs incurred at particular point
  - If units reached that point—Equivalent units = Units × 100%
  - If units haven't reached that point—Equivalent units = Units × 0%

Process Costing (continued)

Process costing—**weighted-average**

1.   Costs in beginning WIP
   + Costs incurred during period
   = Total costs to be allocated

2.   Units completed during period
   + Equivalent units in ending WIP
   = Total equivalent production

3.   Total costs to be allocated
   ÷ Total equivalent production
   = Average cost per equivalent unit

4.   Units completed during period
   × Average cost per equivalent unit
   = Amount allocated to finished goods

5.   Equivalent units in ending inventory
   × Average cost per equivalent unit
   = Amount allocated to ending WIP

Process Costing (continued)

Process costing—**FIFO**

1.   Determine costs incurred during period

2.   Units in beginning WIP
    - − Equivalent units in beginning WIP
    - = Equivalent units required to complete beginning WIP

3.   Equivalent units required to complete beginning WIP
    - ÷ Units started and completed during period × 100%
    - + Equivalent units in ending WIP
    - = Total equivalent production

Process Costing (continued)

4.   Costs incurred during period

   ÷ Total equivalent production

   = Average cost per equivalent unit

5.   Costs in beginning WIP

   + Units started and completed × Average cost per equivalent unit

   = Amount allocated to finished goods

6.   Equivalent units in ending WIP

   × Average cost per equivalent unit

   = Amount allocated to ending WIP

Joint and By-Product Costing

Joint Product Costing

Joint products—two or more products resulting from same process

- **Joint product costs**—costs incurred before products separated
- **Split-off point**—earliest point at which products can be separated
- **Sales value**—amount each product can be sold for at earliest point of sale
- **Separable costs**—costs incurred after split-off point before products can be sold
- **Relative sales value**—Sales value—Separable costs

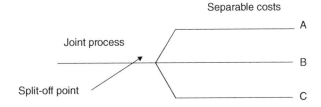

Joint Product Costing (continued)

Allocating joint product costs—relative sales value method

1. Calculate relative sales value for each joint product
2. Add together to calculate total relative sales value
3. Calculate ratio of relative sales value for each joint product to total relative sales value
4. Multiply ratio for each product by joint product costs
5. Result is amount of joint product costs to be allocated to each product

Accounting for By-Products

Revenues from sale of by-products generally reduce cost of other products

1. Determine revenues from sale of by-products
2. Reduce by separable costs, if any, and costs of disposal
3. Net amount reduces cost of primary product or joint costs

Budgeting

Used to estimate revenue, costs, a group of costs, or profits at various levels of activity

- Applies when operating within a relevant range
- Total fixed costs remain the same at all levels within range
- Variable costs per unit of activity remains the same within range

Master and Static Budgets

Static budget—Budget for a specific level of activity

- Can be for division of company
- Can be for company as a whole

Master budget—Static budget for company as a whole

Master budget generally includes:

- Operating budget
- Budgeted cash flows
- Budgeted financial statements

Preparing a Master Budget

1. Estimate sales volume
2. Use sales volume to estimate revenues
3. Use collection history to estimate collections
4. Estimate cost of sales based on units sold
5. Use current finished goods inventory, budgeted ending inventory, and cost of sales to estimate units to be manufactured
6. Use units manufactured to estimate material needs, labor costs, and overhead costs
7. Use material needs, current raw materials inventory, and budgeted ending inventory to budget purchases
8. Use purchase terms to estimate payments
9. Analyze expense and payment patterns to complete operating and cash flow budgets

Budgeting Material Purchases and Payments

	Units sold
+	Budgeted increase in finished goods
−	Budgeted decrease in finished goods
=	Units to be manufactured
×	Units of raw material per unit of finished goods
=	Units of raw material required for production
+	Budgeted increase in raw materials
−	Budgeted decrease in raw materials
=	**Budgeted raw material purchases**
+	Budgeted decrease in accounts payable
−	Budgeted increase in accounts payable
=	**Budgeted payments for raw materials**

Sales and Direct Cost Variance

Material Variances

Standard cost (Units produced × Std qty per unit × Std cost per unit)
  – Actual material cost
  = Total material variance

                      Material price variance (MPV)
                    + Material usage variance (MUV)
                    = Total material variance

MPV = Actual qty × (Std pr – Actual pr)   MUV = Std pr × (Std qty – Actual qty)

Sales and Direct Cost Variance (continued)

Labor Variances

Standard cost (Units produced × Std hrs per unit × Std rate per hr)
    − Actual labor cost
    = Total labor variance

                   Labor rate variance (LRV)
                + Labor efficiency variance (LEV)
                = Total labor variance

LRV = Actual qty × (Std rate − Actual rate)   LEV = Std rate × (Std hrs − Actual hrs)

Overhead Variance Analysis

Overhead Variances

Overhead applied (Std hrs × Total POHR)
− Actual overhead cost
= Total overhead variance

Overhead volume variance (OVV)
+ Overhead efficiency variance (OEV)
+ Overhead spending variance (OSV)
= Total overhead variance

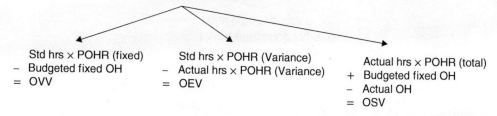

Std hrs × POHR (fixed)
− Budgeted fixed OH
= OVV

Std hrs × POHR (Variance)
− Actual hrs × POHR (Variance)
= OEV

Actual hrs × POHR (total)
+ Budgeted fixed OH
− Actual OH
= OSV

Forecasting Techniques

Sensitivity analysis used to evaluate results of decisions under various conditions

Probability Analysis

Long-term average result (expected value) of decision is estimated

1. Each possible outcome of decision is assigned a probability
2. Total of probabilities is 100%
3. Profit or loss under each possible outcome is determined
4. Profit or loss for outcome multiplied by probability
5. Total of results is added
6. Result is long-term average result

Relevant Costs 1 & 2

Increase or decrease in profits or costs resulting from decision is analyzed

1. Determine increase or decrease in revenues that will result from decision
2. Determine increase or decrease in variable costs that will result from decision
3. Determine if decision will affect fixed costs
4. Net of change in revenues, variable costs, and fixed costs is relevant cost of making decision

Lease versus Buy: Compare Both Options Using Discounted Cash Flow

1. Leasing may require lower initial investment
2. Operating leases off balance sheet
3. Capital leases shift risk of ownership from lessor to lessee

Regression Analysis

Coefficient of correlation (R) indicates relationship between dependent and independent variable:

- R = 1   Strong direct relationship
- 1 > R > 0   Direct relationship, not as strong
- R = 0   No relationship
- 0 > R > –1   Indirect relationship, not as strong
- R = –1   Strong indirect relationship

Company will use cost driver with strongest direct or indirect relationship

Cost-Volume-Profit (Breakeven) Analysis Calculations

Sales price per unit
− Variable cost per unit
= Contrib margin per unit

Contrib margin per unit
÷ Sales price per unit
= Contrib margin ratio

Units

Breakeven

Fixed costs
÷ Contrib margin per unit
= Breakeven in units

Profit as fixed amount

Fixed costs + Desired profit
÷ Contrib margin per unit
= Units required to earn desired profit

Profit as percentage of sales

Fixed costs
÷ Contrib margin − Profit per unit
= Units required to earn profit ratio

Dollars

Fixed costs
÷ Contrib margin ratio
= Breakeven in dollars

Fixed costs + Desired profit
÷ Contrib margin ratio
= Sales dollars required to earn desired profit

Fixed costs
÷ (Contrib margin − Profit) ÷ Sales price
= Sales required to earn profit ratio

Graphical Approach to Breakeven

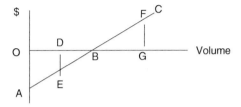

```
AC       = Profit for product at various levels of production
B        = Breakeven point
OA       = Fixed costs
DE       = Loss at production point D (below breakeven)
FG       = Profit at production point G (above breakeven)
OA ÷ OB  = Contribution margin
FG ÷ BG  = Contribution margin
```

Transfer Pricing and Benchmarking

Transfer price—price at which products are transferred from one department to another within the same company

Possible transfer prices:

- Actual cost
- Market value
- Cost + profit
- Negotiated amount
- Standard cost

Transfer from cost center to profit center—generally use standard variable cost

- Cost center evaluated based on comparing standard variable cost to actual cost
- Profit center not affected by performance of cost center

Measurement Frameworks

Balanced scorecards attempt to translate an organization's goals into specific measures with four perspectives:

1. **Financial**—Return on investment and related financial measures
2. **Customer**—Nonfinancial measures of customer satisfaction and retention
3. **Internal business processes**—Measures operating effectiveness and efficiency including financial measures, such as cost variances, and nonfinancial measures, such as number of defects in production
4. **Learning and growth**—Measures employee satisfaction, training, and advancement

Value-based management examines all aspects of a company with the intention of identifying the amount of **economic value added (EVA)** by different activities. In effect, it attempts to translate all activities into their financial value to the firm, and is comparable to a financial scorecard focus.

Balanced Scorecard and Benchmarking

The components of a balanced scorecard include:

- **Strategic objectives**—A statement of the goals of the firm and necessary elements
- **Performance measures**—Identification of quantitative methods that can be used to track success in fulfilling the strategic objectives
- **Baseline performance**—The current level of performance for each measure
- **Targets**—The level or improvement in performance being sought
- **Strategic initiatives**—Programs that will help achieve the targets and objectives

Cause-and-effect linkages identify which performance measures are **performance drivers** (leading indicators) and which are **outcome performance measures** (lagging indicators). This allows the firm to focus on those drivers that are critical to strategic objectives.

Strategy maps are diagrams that identify cause-and-effect linkages:

Value-Based Management

Return on Investment (based on assets) = Net income / Total assets

DuPont return on investment (ROI) analysis: ROI = Return on sales × Asset turnover

- **Return on sales** = Net income / Sales
- **Asset turnover** = Sales / Total assets

Residual income = Operating profit – Interest on investment

- **Interest on investment** = Invested capital × Required rate of return

Economic Value Added: EVA = Net operating profit after taxes (NOPAT) – Cost of financing

- **Cost of financing** = (Total assets – Current liabilities) × Weighted-average cost of capital

Free Cash Flow = NOPAT + Depreciation + Amortization – Capital expenditures – Net increase in working capital

Business Process Management: Focus on Continuous Improvement in Processes to Meet Customers' Needs

Business Processes: Assets in Themselves

1. Design: Identify existing processes/possible improvements
2. Modeling: What-if analysis
3. Execution
   a. Install new software
   b. Test
   c. Train employees
   d. Implement new processes
4. Monitor with performance statistics
5. Optimize
   a. Use performance statistics to identify bottlenecks
   b. Consider strategies (e.g., outsourcing) to remove bottlenecks

Business Process Management: Focus on Continuous Improvement in Processes to Meet Customers' Needs (continued)

6. Other techniques
   a. Reengineer
   b. Lean manufacturing (shorten time by eliminating waste)
   c. Theory of constraints: Increase throughput contribution margin by decreasing investment and operating costs. Must identify and remediate:
      1) Bottleneck resources: capacity is less than demand
      2) Non-bottleneck resources: capacity greater than demand
7. Workflow analysis: Focus on eliminating non-value-added activities

Project Management and Benchmarking

A project is a series of activities and tasks that

- Have specific definable objectives
- Have defined start and end dates
- Are subject to funding constraints
- Consume resources, people, equipment, etc.
- Cut across various functional areas of the organization

Effective project management: Four basic elements

1. Resources
2. Time
3. Money
4. Scope

Project Management and Benchmarking (continued)

Effective project management: Five processes/cycles

1. Project initiation
   a. Support of management
   b. Project manager with authority
   c. Project charter

2. Project planning
   a. Define scope
   b. Identify resources needed
   c. Schedule tasks
   d. Identify risks

Project Management and Benchmarking (continued)

3. Project execution
   a. Managing work
   b. Directing team
4. Project monitoring and control
   a. Tracking progress
   b. Comparing actual outcomes to predicted outcomes (variances)
5. Project closure

Project Management Tools

1. Life-cycle approach: Define and assess each phase of project
2. Gantt chart—bar chart that illustrates the scheduled start and finish of elements of a project over time

Project Management and Benchmarking (continued)

3. Program Evaluation and Review Technique (PERT): Focus on the interdependency of activities and the time required to complete an activity to schedule and control the project
   a. Critical path: The shortest amount of time necessary to accomplish the project.
      1) Optimistic
      2) Most likely
      3) Pessimistic
4. PERT used where there is a high variability of completion time, such as R&D
5. ABC analysis: Categorize tasks into three groups:
   a. Tasks that are perceived as being urgent and important
   b. Tasks that are important but not urgent
   c. Tasks that are neither urgent nor important

INDEX

Index